GEORGE CAPPANNELLI

We The People - Democracy's Best and Last Hope

21 Ways To Save America From Tyranny

First published by On Life Publising 2025

Copyright © 2025 by George Cappannelli

All rights reserved. No part of this publication may be reproduced, stored or transmitted in any form or by any means, electronic, mechanical, photocopying, recording, scanning, or otherwise without written permission from the publisher. It is illegal to copy this book, post it to a website, or distribute it by any other means without permission.

Cover Design – George Cappanelli

First edition

ISBN: 978-0-9623108-2-9

This book was professionally typeset on Reedsy. Find out more at reedsy.com

*"We are born to be the architects
of the future, not its victims."*
– R.Buckminster Fuller

Contents

Preface	ii
Chapter One - A Call To Patriotism	1
Chapter Two - Framing The Dilemma	13
Chapter Three - A Little Back Story	35
Chapter Four - Revisiting The Threat	43
Chapter Five- The Disease of The Soul	55
Chapter Six - Creating A United Front	64
Chapter Seven - Eleven Individual Keys and Cures	69
Chapter Eight - Ten Collective Keys and Cures	85
Chapter Nine - Just A Few More Things	97
Chapter Ten - Next Steps & Special Bonuses	102
Chapter Eleven - About The Author	108
Chapter Twelve - The Declaration of Independence	111
Afterword	119

Preface

PRAISE FOR THE AUTHOR'S WORK

"Real answers for individuals and a world—in crisis"
Radio TV Interview Report

"This inspiring book is filled with valuable insights to move you forward, step by step to a place where you can enthusiastically make successful change."
NAPRA Review

"Profound, compassionate, and deeply useful, Do Not Go Quietly is a guide to the genius and capacities inherent in the second half of life. It brooks no whiney nay-saying but rather offers a repositioning of the senior in our time. Seniors become the midwives of souls, the evocators of self and society."

Jean Houston, Best Selling Author

"These are challenging times. We are being asked to do more, oftentimes with fewer people and less resources. Change is a constant factor in our lives, and we can use all the help we can get. We have used many of the concepts that George & Sedena Cappannelli discuss in Say Yes to Change. They are valuable."

Brewster Shaw, Boeing Program Manager, International Space Station, former Chief of U.S. Astronauts

In Do Not Go Quietly, the Cappannellis remind us that the road to a more conscious future passes directly through the process of harvesting the wisdom and experience of our past and participating individually and collectively in writing a new 'third act' for the future."

Rabbi Zalman Schachter-Shalomi, author of Age-ing To Sage-ing.

"George Cappannelli helped us meet our current and future workload by creating a new operating state that improves trust and teamwork and propels our vision."

General Donald Cromer, President, Hughes Space & Communications

"Authenticity is a terrific book for our times! George and Sedena Cappannelli are 'truth-tellers who have written a gem of a book."

The Very Reverend Edward, II Harrison, Dean of St John's Cathedral

"Millions of Cultural Creatives are both changing their lives and creating a new culture in response to the crises of our age. This book offers a wise, no-frills, practical way to do your Inner Work. Try this book, you need it." Paul H. Ray, Ph.D., coauthor of The Cultural Creatives

"George and Sedena have written a thoughtful, thorough, and surprising book on the wisdom of aging. Do Not Go Quietly inspires and encourages us to live fully at any age; to act boldly for the sake of the world as well as for our own souls."
Michael Meade, Best Selling Author, Mythologist, Poet, and Story Teller

" The Cappannellis are the real deal. Their coaching work with world-class organizations and high-performing individuals gets to the heart of the matter."

Melina Borrows, Contributing Writer at Cosmopolitan, Ladies Home Journal.

Chapter One - A Call To Patriotism

> "The superior man seeks
> what is right,
> The inferior man
> what is profitable"
> -Confucious

A Call To Patriotism In A Time of Tyranny

Our nation is under attack from within and this attack represents the most egregious threat to our democracy and our way of life in our 248+ year history. As a result of the scope and intensity of this attack and the current disruption and dysfunction in our government, I believe We the People constitute democracy's best and last hope.

So, I invite you to take a journey with me to discover if this is true for you as well, and if it is, what we, as citizens and members of the Fifth Estate, can do individually and jointly to stop this all-out attempt by these men and women who call themselves MAGA Republicans and who I believe have lost their way, to rob us of our sovereignty, desecrate our rights, and freedoms, and destroy our way of life.

Of course, since I began writing this book immediately following the election, a great deal has changed. It appears to me that the shock, confusion, disbelief, and anger that marked my initial response to Donald Trump's win, and that seemed to mirror the experience of many of us here in this country and around the world, is thankfully being replaced by the admission that something is very wrong. It is also being replaced by the re-emergence of signs of that indomitable will and courage that has, at many other critical times in our history, proven to be the hallmark of the American spirit.

Indeed, the more unconscious and negative the actions of the current Trump administration become, the more draconian and unjustified their firings of Federal employees, the more dangerous their reduction and elimination of our essential services, the larger the number of valued agencies and programs that are tbeing threatened or hollowed out from within, the more our relationships with our neighbors and allies are being negatively impacted, the more the free press is attacked, law firms threatened, and efforts made to intimidate our universities, colleges, and students, the more this administration moves to exact vengeance against individuals whose only so-called crime has been to do their best to hold this President and his syncophants accountable for their many crimes and violations of the Rule of Law, the more he attempts to impose his brand of dangerous and chaotic tariffs that negatively impact our financial markets and that of the world, as well as our relationships with friends and allies and our adversaries and the cost of living for all Americans, the more inhumane and arbitrary this administration's deportation initiative becomes, the more pronounced this president's support of Putin and Russia rather than Ukraine and our Western Allies becomes... etc..., etc..., etc..., the more we as citizens all across the country are waking up to the severity of the threat this president and his sycophants pose.

This re-emergence of our willingness to defend our democracy was also demonstrated recently when We the People turned out to vote in significant numbers in the special elections in Florida and Wisconsin, and on April 5th, the first national Hands-Off Day of Protests when an estimated 5 million people came out into the streets in towns and cities all across the country to voice our concerns, fears, and, objections to the current actions as well as to the announced future intentions of this administration, the mind-numbing incompetence of the members of the new cabinet this President has appointed, and the deafening silence and gross abdication of responsibilities being demonstrated by the MAGA members in Congress, that is supposed to be a discerning, powerful co-equal branch of government in our unique system of checks and balances.

This exercise of our right to free speech and our right to protest has, in some valuable ways, focused attention on some of these abuses, and signaled to other citizens and to our friends and allies in other countries that We the People have not lost our minds. These protests have also helped to impact or, at the least, delay or lessen some of the damage this administration has tried to impose on our government and our way of life. And yet, from my perspective, the current blitzkrieg on our democracy in the form of the roll-out of Project 2025 continues largely unabated, as does this administration's commitment to turn our democracy into a bastardized version of an autocratic kleptocracy and a White Nationalist state.

Time To Up The Ante

For this reason, I believe it is time that We the People significantly up the ante in our response to this egregious threat before the damage created by these conmen and incompetents steals our fate. And I believe we can do this best by organizing and executing a National Campaign of Resolve dedicated to saving our democracy. We can do this best by utilizing all of our precious, God-given, unalienable rights, freedoms, and responsibilities - and most particularly, those that can have a major economic impact on this administration including - work slowdowns, boycotts, rolling general strikes, and even temporary tax withholding revolts, yes even temporary tax withhold revolts. After all, if this lawless administration believes it has the right to hollow out our government agencies, fire thousands of Federal workers, significantly reduce or eliminate essential services without our permission, and violate the right to due process of legal residents as a precursor to doing this to citizens, it seems that We the People should explore the right to stop paying our taxes, at least, until this abuse and gross disregard stop.

I believe, therefore, that these forms of economic protest, added to our traditional use of petitions, phone calls, emails, texts, letters to the editor, office visits to our representatives, and our demands for public town halls and marches, will greatly advance our efforts to defend our democracy against those committed to its destruction. And, the sooner we execute a coordinated National Campaign of Resolve and utilize these powerful forms of economic protest and do so, not only by the hundreds, but the hundreds of thousands and hopefully, as we demonstrated on April 5th of this year, by the many millions, the better off we and our country will be.

I also stress the need to do all of this non-violently - otherwise, this administration will find the justification they are currently looking for to release the dogs of war on us. I also believe we should exercise all of our unalienable rights and execute the National Campaign out of our love for our democracy and our way of life and not in hate or anger against those who are intent on harming us. And the sooner we do this the sooner we will begin to see many of the major and positive results we seek.

So I ask you to pause for a moment and picture this in your mind. Picture millions of us in the streets all across the country, and most especially in Washington, on the Washington Moment Mall, encircling the White House, the Capital, the various House and Senate Office Buildings, and The Supreme Court. Not blocking roads, not obstructing flow in and. out, but peacefully, at times perhaps, even silently. I also ask you to envision this happening not just for a day, or two but every day, silently, non-violently, and consistently until these individuals who are intent on destroying our country acknowledge that We the People will not sit idly by and allow them to destroy our country, take away all of our freedoms, rights, and responsibilities and destroy our dreams and aspirations, as well s those of our children, grandchildren and all future generations.

And, this is not to say we should stop our efforts to identify the very best candidates, create new and highly effective communication strategies, develop the best ground games, and defend against the many efforts to limit or prevent voter turnout in preparation for the mid-term elections. These are all important and necessary things. However, when I consider the severity and scope of the threat we face, I believe we would be naive to bet the entire farm on future elections alone, especially when those who are out to destroy us control the White House, both Houses of Congress, the majority of Justices on the Supreme Court and a significant number of state legislatures.

Other Considerations

So at this critical time, let us keep our eyes fixed firmly on the goal of taking back our country. And, to this end, it is essential that we not lose sight of a fundamental truth, one that I fear we too often seem to forget. THIS IS OUR COUNTRY! It does not belong to an ex-real state developer with an oversized ego and a malicious and insatiable fantasy about being king. Nor is it some billionaire's personal playground. Nor does it belong to the rag-tag group of obsequious cabinet members this president has appointed, nor to the MAGA members of Congress or the MAGA majority on the Supreme Court who lack the character, philosophical grounding, and independence of thought, action, and integrity required to uphold their oaths of office and serve the well-being of all of the people of this nation.

Our country is both a Constitutional Republic and a Representative Democracy. It is not, and if we do our job will never be an autocracy, kleptocracy, or theocracy. Our country, the United States of America, was formed in protest of a king, his arbitrary and unfair taxation, his absurd belief that he ruled by divine right, and his refusal to honor the right of people in a new land to have a genuine voice in determining their fate. Our country was birthed in keeping with the Laws of Nature and the Laws of God and of, by, and for We the People. And this was made abundantly clear when our founders declared that "all men are created equal," which means not just MAGA Republicans and White Nationalists, not just the wealthy, the obsequious, those hypnotized by their lust for power, or cowered by their fear of retribution. It means all men, all women, and all children. So let us remember that these United States of America belong to us and that we are endowed, not by man, but by our creator "with certain unalienable rights, and that among them are Life, Liberty, and the pursuit of Happiness."

Let us also keep another fundamental truth close at hand. Let us remember to heed this warning issued long ago by Saint Augustine.

"He who created us without our help, will not save us without our consent."

Not A Time To Hesitate

Another very important consideration, from my perspective, is that we do not have time to procrastinate, equivocate, hesitate, fall victim to the belief that "it can't happen here," or settle for only partial and temporary solutions. Nor should we be pacified or misled by what those in this administration say or promise. Based on the transition from what was promised in the campaign to what has been acted out since this administration assumed office, there should be little doubt in any of our minds, even those who rabidly and unconsciously defend this administration, that this president and his minions cannot be trusted.

So it is my recommendation that we not only look but see, not only listen but hear, and not only feel, but follow the wisdom of our hearts and that still small voice within that speaks clearly to the fact that this travesty, this attempt to steal our nation from us, is already happening, and there are things we are being called to do now to prevent it.

We would also be wise to remember that democracy is more than just a form of government or a political process, it is a sacred trust that We the People have been entrusted with. It is, as the great books of wisdom confirm, the truest and most direct path we can walk on toward higher levels of consciousness, concepts of legitimate individual empowerment and mutual responsibility, greater cooperation, compassion, and integrity. Democracy is the path we can walk on in honor of those who have come before us and on whose shoulders we stand. It is the path that allows us to give inspiration and hope to those who are also alive at this time on this planet and who have not yet had the opportunity to experience the extraordinary gift of living in a nation free of tyranny. And of special consequence, it gives those of us who are citizens the most remarkable gift of being stewards of these rights and freedoms for those not yet born and who, if we act with courage and purpose, will have the opportunity to take their turn at working with this still imperfect 248+ year experiment to that create that long-promised, more perfect union.

So as we journey together toward this goal of saving our democracy together, I will do my best to explore the nature of the threat we face in greater detail. I will also say more about the "Disease of the Soul/Virus of the Mind that was identified long ago by our Algonquin, Cree, and Ojibway brothers and sisters, and more recently, by C G Jung as a result of his study of the rise and fall of the Nazi scourge and how this disease has now unfortunately afflicted many of those who are determined to visit their destruction upon us.

I will also spend some time in these pages exploring what I believe needs to be another essential part of our defense of democracy. And that is the need to create a common front comprised of all of our activist, advocacy, and legal defense organizations, our past and current duly elected and appointed leaders who still support our Constitution and our system of checks and balances, our labor unions who have not sold out to those who would oppress us, our academic institutions who are holding firm to their mission of preserving freedom of thought and preparing our young people some to create a remarkable future, members of the free press that shine a light on the travesty, of valued law firms that defend our rights and freedoms, historians, scholars, scientists, and experts who offer us clarity and who can help We the People strategize, organize and act in concert and in a timely way to defend and support issues, policies, and initiatives of vital importance. It is this united front that I believe can successfully execute the National Campaign Of Resolve To Save Our Democracy.

Along the way, I will do my best to identify what I believe the role of the Democratic Party needs to be, as well as things Republicans, Independents, Libertarians, and even people who do not choose to affiliate with any political party, but who value both our democracy and our way of life can do. And to the best of my ability, I will avoid using a lot of our precious time trying to relitigate the 2024 election. For, on one hand, what is done is done. Although, I have to admit I sincerely regret that the Democrats did not, at the very least, contest the 2024 election results in the seven swing states. I say this because, from my perspective, the results were a little too perfect and convenient. Plus, when I consider how much pain and suffering Donald Trump imposed on our nation with his false claims known as the Big Lie that claimed the 2020 election was stolen, I believe, it would only have been just, at the very least, to return the favor.

It is also telling from my standpoint, that Donald Trump and his sycophants and most assuredly those in the shadows behind them were able to come out of the gate right after the election and begin implementing this blitzkrieg called Project 2025. While I know that some of them spent the preceding four years planning this catastrophe, it still seems to me that there was something they knew that the rest of us did not. Which, in my mind, increases the likelihood that there was some kind of sophisticated and malicious election interference involved. This is also the case when I think back to that period late in the campaign when Donald Trump began boasting that he didn't need any more votes. I remember wondering if all of that was just another of his many empty boasts, or if it was Donald Trump - the wounded child with the exaggerated ego - who simply could not keep himself from gloating in advance and aloud about the actions that he knew were being taken by others behind the scenes - both foreign and domestic - to manufacture his victory.

Unfortunately, thanks to the Democrats' lack of effective strategic, political planning during the four years when they controlled first the White House, the House, and the Senate, and then the White House and the Senate, and then when they demonstrated their misguided belief after their loss in November that they would somehow benefit by adopting the role of the good Boy Scouts and play softball in a hardball league. This same miscalculation was apparent when the very best the Democrats could do in protest of the avalanche of lies and misinformation Donald Trump delivered in his first message before the joint session of Congress was to hold up little cardboard paddles that looked ridiculously like polite attempts to request permission to go to the bathroom. They also had no impact whatsoever on the content Trump was delivering, his disdain for them, or his ongoing assault on truth. And to make matters worse, instead of celebrating the courage of the one member of the House, Congressman Green from Texas, who stood up and called out the President for his assault on truth, ten of the prissy alter boys in the Democratic Party joined the rapid MAGA Republicans in the house in censuring Congressman Green.

As a result of these misguided and non-strategic actions, it has become clear to me, and now thankfully, to a growing number of us that the Democratic leadership in Washington lacks both courage and the will to move past old thinking and impotent actions. For, although the members of this leadership team have spent hours trying to justify their actions, I believe our nation lost a valuable opportunity to discover if the 2024 election was rigged, and if so, how. The Democrats also lost an even more important opportunity to declare that they were not just the minority party, but "the opposition party," and that they would represent We the People and stand up against the tide of chaos, confusion, and abuse of our way of life, uphold our core values and the Rule of Law, and protect and defend our Constitution.

And, please, do not pass too quickly over this distinction between a minority party and the "opposition party. The term "minority party" implies business as usual, particularly in a two-party system that has taken for granted the protection of our checks and balances. Under these and other normal circumstances, one party, perhaps more fiscally conservative and often facing toward the past instead of the future, has generally come into power for several years, and then, there has been a reversal through a legitimate vote by our citizens and the other party, the one more oriented to expanding 'the commons" and looking forward rather than back, has replaced it. And while this vacillation has not always supported the highest and best interests of our nation and certainly not the needs of all of our people, particularly when our political process periodically devolves, as it has recently, into tribal warfare, our normal two-party dance has, at the very least, been a sign of a reasonably stable, if somewhat immature government, in which all parties support the founding documents, and most especially the Constitution and the Rule of Law.

An "opposition party" on the other hand, represents those who are out of power, but it is not docile, patient, and willing to play pattycake with the Majority party, especially in instances when the majority party is corrupt or does not represent the best interests of the people. Under these latter circumstances, the opposition party's job is to focus on organizing, educating, and inspiring We the People to use all of our rights, our strength in numbers, our financial resources, physical labor, as well as, our passion, sense of justice, and commitment to do everything possible to stop, slow down, and when necessary, derail the party in power, when that party demonstrates that it has lost it's way. And that, my fellow, Americans is precisely the role I believe some Democrats like Bernie Sanders and Alexandra Ocassio Cortez, Cory Booker. Chris Murphy and others are thankfully beginning to demonstrate. And, now, it is my fervent hope that all of the Democrats, Independents, Libertarians, and Republicans of conscience will wake up and also start doing their jobs as members of the Opposition Party until justice is served and our nation returns to sanity.

Additional Goals

It is also not the goal of this book to attempt to cover all of the ground explored by legitimate members of the media who have and are continuing to do a herculean job in uncovering and exposing many of the President's crimes and over-reach. However, I believe that at this time when information is being presented in so many different formats on many different platforms, when the truth is greatly abused and too often proves to be sadly illusive, and when a significant number of people are being intentionally lied to and misdirected by this President and the rag-tag members of his embarrassingly incompetent administration, as well the MAGA members who have lost not only their integrity but even their voice, it is necessary to keep the record straight, and essential to prevent our free press to uphold their responsibilities as ABC, CBS did not do in settling bogus lawsuits and The Washington Post did not do in announcing a change in its editorial policy that has some of its most long-standing and courageous journalists announcing their resignations. Not an easy task when we have a president who is undoubtedly one of the most accomplished media manipulators of all time and also the most prolific deceiver to have ever occupied the White House.

This situation is exacerbated, of course, by the unprecedented number of ethically compromised MAGA sycophants currently in Congress and the equally large number of corrupt members of the FOX national media organization who appear to be so lacking in integrity and human decency that they are immune to feeling shame as they continue their efforts to deceive the American people. Then, there are the troll farms and other major disruptors run by the Russians and the Chinese and more often these days by Iran and North Korea as well. For this reason, I believe, it is essential to take some time in this book to better define the nature and scope of this threat Donald Trump and the malevolents who support him now pose to our nation.

It is also the goal of this book to identify additional root causes that also are the result of things We the People failed to do - fulfill our civic duties and responsibilities as citizens - as well as our failure to demonstrate sufficient levels of ethical and moral standards and demand the same of our leaders. So I will take the time to do that here on these pages because I believe these failures have contributed, at least as much as Donald Trump's deceit, to the travesty we now face.

Finally, it is also my intent to use the pages of this book to identify 21 powerful, effective, and readily available keys and cures We the People can use with deep commitment, genuine passion and integrity, and above all with an understanding of what is required of us to turn back this Philistines and defend our way of life and our form of government.

Chapter Two - Framing The Dilemma

> "No matter how noble the objectives of a government,
> if it blurs decency and kindness, cheapens human life,
> and breeds ill will and suspicion,
> it is an evil government."
> - Eric Hoffer

The Dilemma

With these goals in mind, I invite you to pay special attention to the quote above. Eric Hoffer, a former longshoreman, American social critic, and philosopher, was awarded our nation's highest civilian honor, the Presidential Medal of Freedom, a year before he died in 1982 and long before Donald Trump, who lies at the center of this most egregious current threat to our democracy, came on the national political scene.

Yet, with surgical insight, undeniable clarity, and a heartfelt frankness, Hoffer managed in just 23 words to define the essential difference between an enlightened and constructive government committed to the genuine advancement and well-being of all of its people for the greater good and an evil government whose focus is on manipulating and subjugating its people for its own selfish and malevolent ends.

Unfortunately, the historical record shows that there have been far more governments that meet Eric Hoffer's definition of evil than governments that qualify as enlightened. It is also clear that these evil governments have kept humanity mired in cycles of tyranny, regression, enormous loss of human life, incalculable amounts of suffering and destruction, and the domination of the many by the few. And, this reality makes the rise of autocratic governments in our time confounding and disturbing and prompts me to wonder if our species has learned anything at all from these past cycles of chaos.

It is also sad but true, that our democracy, even with its noble beginnings and its proud claims of freedoms and rights, has been responsible for a number of policies and actions executed both within our borders against segments of our population and beyond our borders against people in other lands, that qualify us, at least periodically, for membership in Hoffer's evil category.

And on the matter of this current threat against our democracy, which is the core topic of this book, using these criteria Hoffer identified, it is clear to me that the 2nd Trump administration certainly qualifies as a truly evil government. And I am moved to say this not just as a result of this administration's early actions, but because of its stated intention, its lack of compassion, its commitment to cruelty and revenge, and its long-term objective of doing its very best to destroy this remarkable nation.

What reinforces this conclusion and what is particularly dangerous and troubling about this current threat is that it is being advanced by people who claim to be loyal Americans committed to working on behalf of We the People to make America great again. Unfortunately for us, both of these claims are fraudulent. First, these individuals are not loyal Americans. Based on their current behavior, their deception, and the destruction they are visiting upon our people, our government, as well as our relationships with countries that have been our friends and faithful allies for so long, I do not believe they even qualify any longer to be called citizens. Instead, they are wolves in sheep's clothing committed to destroying America from within for their gain and the benefit of our enemies.

Their claim that they are committed to making America great again is also patently false. Indeed, it is a thinly veiled cover story for the major deception and misdirection they have used to erode trust in our government, divide our people, and are now using to undercut our commitment to the policies and practices that have made our nation the envy of the world.

Interestingly enough, this aspect of the MAGA lie is easily refuted. However, it takes a willingness to open our eyes, our ears, and our hearts and to acknowledge the facts and the data that support them. If we do these things we will have only one choice - to acknowledge that until January 20, 2024, our country was not failing, as the Trump campaign fraudulently claimed and as the Trump administration continues to claim. Instead, our country was on a very positive trajectory and doing remarkably well, especially when compared to the vast majority of other countries in the world.

The Tale of The Tape

Under the Biden Administration, we had turned the corner faster and better than any other country in the world leaving behind both the ravages of the pandemic and the chaos, the failed policies and attempted coup advanced by the first Trump Administration. As a result, we had the most thriving economy in the world, And thanks to a stable and very experienced government, we had largely repaired the damage done to our national agencies and structure under Trump, rebuilt strong and constructive relationships with most of our Western allies and were taking solid steps to form new and equally healthy alliances with countries in the Pacific and the Far East. For the first time in decades, we were also making some progress on gun control – certainly not enough, of course, but more than we had in 30 years, and also on actually bringing rather than just promising to bring manufacturing back within our borders.

Under the Biden Administration, America had turned the corner faster and better than any other country after leaving behind the ravages of the pandemic. It also brought us stability and sanity after the period of chaos and confusion caused by Donald Trump's erratic nature during his first administration, as well as a result of his many failed domestic policies. For example, this self-proclaimed business genius inherited a very robust and vibrant economy from the Obama Administration and, in no time at all, managed to infuse it with chaos, confusion, and instability.

Donald Trump's disastrous efforts to destroy our relationships with our allies and his obsequious need to kneel to Putin even though the dictator had launched an unprovoked invasion of Ukraine and had been a declared enemy of the United States for over 70 years.

All of this and the disruption and shock caused his bungling of the Covid Crisis and the attempted coup executed at his direction by a previous collection of individuals of questionable character and competency whose loyalty was never to our nation and our form of government but exclusively to this disturbed and disaffected individual who for reasons beyond comprehension, they still worship.

By comparison, under the Biden Administration, we witnessed the remarkable repair of in a relatively short time of the damage done to our national agencies and structure under Trump in a very short time. The Biden administration also rebuilt strong and constructive relationships with most of our Western allies and also took meaningful steps to form new and equally healthy alliances with countries in the Pacific and the Far East. For the first time in decades, we also making some progress on gun control – certainly not enough, of course, but more than we had in 30 years, and also on actually bringing rather than just promising to bring manufacturing back within our borders.

The Biden administration also successfully initiated a major and long-needed infrastructure repair and new construction program, and although not yet enough and with a badly divided and highly partisan Congress, managed to launch new policies that both acknowledged and committed us to do some much-needed work to slow down, if not to fully address, the coming climate catastrophes.

America was, therefore, most assuredly not failing as Donald Trump falsely and repeatedly claimed during the campaign and continues to claim in the early days of this administration. And this is not to say that the Biden Administration did everything right. Among the major flies in the ointment was the fact that although inflation was under control, employment numbers strong, and there were early signs of lower interest rates, consumer prices, particularly in the grocery aisles, were still too high. Immigration, on our southern border which had been broken for decades, was not improved, and in some ways, was exacerbated under Biden.

While the Biden administration did many things of real and necessary value in support of Ukraine and NATO, and although there were gains made on the battlefield by Ukraine, the US failed to supply the kind of weapons that were needed early enough and in large enough quantities to allow Ukraine to capitalize on Russia's obvious military weakness. It was also true that the war was very costly and there was no end yet in sight. I

There was also the situation in Gaza that had become unacceptable. This was, I believe largely due to Israel's recalcitrant right-wing Prime Minister who himself was trying to escape criminal prosecution, and a radically conservative right-wing segment of the cabinet whose only interest was settlement expansion and the prevention of a legitimate two-state solution. But these objectives were, of course, as they always are, hidden beneath the rhetoric of war, revenge for the indiscriminate slaughter of Israeli civilians, and the taking of hostages. Although, it has been abundantly clear that the Prime Minister and the far-right members of the cabinet have, from the beginning, been far more focused on destroying not just Humas but Gaza itself, than on ensuring the return of the hostages.

It is also true that our long-term commitment to Israel's defense involved our providing them with heavy munitions, which they, indiscriminately and unconsciously used to create a heinous and criminal situation in Gaza. The result was the complete physical destruction of Gaza both in the north and the south and an enormous loss of life. But instead of the Prime Minister and the hard right cabinet ministers taking the heat, segments of our population here in the US - most significantly, young people on college campuses and people of Middle Eastern descent - directed their ire toward Biden, and then began looking for an alternative in the 2024 election. Sadly, when these elements were coupled with our fractured media environment, its unreliable and inaccurate information flow, and a less than effective communications job done by the Biden Administration itself, a significant number of Americans failed to understand how much good had been and was continuing to be done by Biden and his team.

This situation was further compounded by President Biden's physical decline - a thing that was not well explained and that caused additional confusion and concern among a large number of Democratic voters and also among key members of President Biden's party. When compounded by his late decision to withdraw from the race, Kamala Harris was put in the almost impossible position of having to design, organize, and run a full campaign in about 100 days. And while she came very close to pulling off a stunning victory, the haunting specter of misogyny and racism – two of America's most potent and unacceptable remaining prejudices – constituted a vulnerability that not even her artful, effective, and impassioned campaign could overcome.

Misinformation and Unprecedented Deception

Meanwhile, the Trump Campaign was continuing to orchestrate an ugly, but highly effective misinformation and misdirection campaign that was amplified by members of the Republican Party who had been highly critical of Donald Trump four years before and in some notable cases, the current Vice President for one, who did so even more brutally and more recently than that. And yet, in the run-up to the 2024 election, many of these individuals somehow managed to justify their lack of integrity and the sacrifice of their character and values and ended up supporting this Deceiver in Chief. Some, of course, did this out of fear of his reprisals. Others out of greed and their quest for the illusion of power. Still, others were seduced by the belief that, poisonous or not, Donald Trump might well be the answer to their minority party's ability to control the majority. And, since the goal of doing this had been in place since Lewis Powell penned what is now called The Powell Memorandum, in the months before he took his seat as an Associate Justice of the Supreme Court in 1972. This memorandum became the playbook for the conservative wing of the Republican Party, of the Corporate sector, and eventually for the party as a whole.

If my claim sounds preposterous to you, I invite you to take a few moments to google "The Powell Memorandum." I believe you will find that this document gave the Republican Party and the corporate sector a very cunning and effective blueprint that has been used for decades in a stealth effort to undercut the rule of the majority.

There was, however, something else in play, something that I believe accounted for the seemingly irrational and hard-to-explain reversal of the major criticism of Trump advanced by many members of his party and his effectiveness in cultivating what has become known as the MAGA faithful. In Chapter Five, titled, "The Disease of the Soul, I will say more about this factor that I believe has contributed substantially to the travesty now taking place.

Other Contributing Factors

The divisive and destructive messages being advanced by the Trump Campaign and his mimics in Congress were also trumpeted by what is, without a doubt, the most corrupt and devious communication company masquerading as a legitimate news organization in the Western world. This and a whole series of fake social media sites and troll farms were effectively created by the Russians and the Chinese. And in the months leading up to the election, Iran and North Korea also joined this effort. This cacophony of misinformation and deception, coupled with what I believe will someday be uncovered as very significant electronic interference by some yet-to-be-named party, and most particularly in the swing states, contributed to a Trump victory.

This result has proven to be both unfortunate and very dangerous for our country and the world at large. It certainly was not wanted by the millions of us who were and remain very much committed to democracy. But based on the factors identified above, as well as some of the division and incompetence demonstrated by Democrats, the resulting disaffection of some women and a number of men in a badly uninformed and fickled electorate, and what I will call the RFK factor, which brought at least a few million so-called liberals who were seemingly trying desperately to re-live the glory days of the 60's but who, like Bararbas who joined the burning of Rome too late, allowed themselves to be deceived by the one major figure from the Kennedy dynasty who had been disowned by his family and was also ridiculed by the scientific community for many of his questionable beliefs. These factors, and what I contend was some very talented election manipulation, proved to be too much to prevent the then-ex and the now current President from conning enough Americans into giving him another go at the White House so he could continue his quest to be king.

And, while still early in this new administration, we now find ourselves in a situation where all of the criteria so clearly identified by Eric Hoffer in his definition of evil governments are openly in play within our country.

The Oath of Office - A Clear Sign Of Things to Come

Among the actions exhibited by this President in the first months of his 2nd administration, there is one I find particularly distasteful and I believe the majority of us who are citizens should as well. It was also an undeniable sign of the scope of the challenges that lie ahead for our nation.

On January 20th, this President-elect stood before our nation and the entire world and fraudulently took the sacred oath of office mandated by our Constitution.

> **"I do solemnly swear (or affirm) that I will faithfully execute the office of President of the United States, and will to the best of my ability, preserve, protect, and defend the Constitution of the United States. So Help Me God."**

In doing this, Donald Trump not only mocked and dishonored 248+ years of our country's history as well as all of the 45 other Presidents who, as imperfect and compromised as some were, still managed to honor the Constitution. This even includes Richard Nixon, who agreed to resign as a result of his crimes. But Donald Trump simply and boldly continued his habitual and unconscionable act of spreading lies and disinformation. And what made those moments in the Capitol of the United States even more damaging than his false claim that the 2020 election was stolen was that in the Rotunda, the very Rotunda to which he, 4 years before, had sent a highly agitated and angry crowd of thousands of people intent on stopping the certification of the 2020 election results and hopefully launch the overthrow of our government, his blasphemous taking of this sacred oath not only demonstrated his complete lack of ethical standards, it also propelled our nation further into a no man's land of falsehoods and distrust that could very well lead our democracy, if We the People do not wake up in time and do what is needed, to a tragic and ignoble end.

What compounds this danger is the fact that the Vice President also took a sacred oath on January 20, 2024. It was slightly different than the President's but in some ways arguably, even more specific. The same was true for all of the MAGA members of the new Congress who took this second version of the oath when the new Congress convened on January 5th. And in this time and the months ahead, the same will be true when the collection of what is indisputably the most unqualified, incompetent, and emotionally unstable political appointees any President in recent history has made to his cabinet, are confirmed by the 53 MAGA Rubber-Stamp Senators who have abdicated their duty to effectively perform their advise and consent function as members of a co-equal branch of government.

And what makes all of this particularly repugnant is that to a man and woman, these individuals, including the President himself, the Vice President, the MAGA member of Congress, and the new cabinet appointees, are so lacking in character that none among them demonstrated any qualms over taking an oath to defend and protect our Constitution. This is even though they, to a person, are openly committed to doing all in their power to turn our nation into an autocratic kleptocracy and White Christian Nationalist State. And what is truly dangerous about this is that if We the People, do not start exercising our courage and the full scope of our unalienable rights, this MAGA government that has lost both its way and its adherence to truth, may very well succeed in its objective.

What also makes their malicious intent so troubling is that this second attempted coup – the first, of course, being the January 5th, 2020 insurrection with its false claims and false electors scheme– is occurring at a time when the global ecological clock is speeding up dramatically and putting at risk not only the survival of our form of government but all of humanity, all of the other species and this precious habitat that is struggling so mightily to sustain us. And if this possibility doesn't shake all of us who are citizens of this country - indeed, all of the citizens of the world -to our very cores, I am not sure if anything ever will.

A Blitzkrieg of Malevolence

It is also clear to me that the scope and speed of this threat currently being advanced by the Trump Administration, something that only came into full view during the first month of his second term in office, has already violated many of national our core values, qualities of character, ethical and moral standards, traditional norms and standards of behaviors, and above all, the Rule of Law that has served as the foundation for our lives for hundreds of years. As a result, I and, based on current polling, a great number of you, my fellow citizens, have been propelled into a strange limbo of disbelief, confusion. procrastination, and doubt, leaving us without anything familiar to hold onto and, at least for a time, without knowing exactly what to do.

A Potential Upside

There is, however, the possibility, depending on the amount of courage and commitment We the People continue to express in reaction to all of this chaos and misdirection, that this threat will prove to be the much-needed whack on the side of the head we have needed for some time. A wake-up call that could finally prompt us to revisit, refine, renew, and take immediate and specific actions to both defend our way of life and strengthen the essential spirit and intent of this nation that was present at the time of its founding and is so eloquently captured in our founding documents.

On the other hand, these individuals who have lost their way as well as their integrity and any semblance of adherence to truth, appear to be under some form of hypnosis, and like people in a trance, they are now obsessively committed to moving ahead like Trumpian zombies willing to inflict a degree of chaos and harm on both our government and our people that we have never experienced before. And if they continue on this path and remain under this amount of soul-numbing hypnosis, and if We the People do not find a way to deter them, I fear their actions will sound the death knell to our once noble dream and force all of us – including even these bad actors themselves - to take a next and irreversible step on the road to what has been called the Sixth Extinction Event.

The Other Side of The Coin

Eric Hoffer's words, however, also provide us with another opportunity, one that is long overdue. I believe it is an opportunity if we are willing to take advantage of it and use it to not only defend our democracy but to take important steps on the path toward democracy's true promise. These steps involve our finally coming clean on the role we have played, or perhaps it is more accurate to say, failed to play in preventing our nation from committing some of the things that Hoffer describes as evil. And it is these things that I believe have exacerbated the long, slow, and dangerous ethical and moral decline that has led We the People to now be required to face this Trump travesty.

So I believe that no matter how shocked or confused we may be, no matter how disoriented and hesitant, we must find the will, the courage, and the personal and collective integrity to break through any remaining resistance and instead, start using all of our God-given unalienable rights and freedoms, follow the dictates of our hearts rather than the fears and limited beliefs generated in our minds, and, in this way, reclaim our sovereignty and take our country back from those who are intent on destroying it for their own warped goals.

I believe, therefore, that this is the first and the most essential thing We the People must do to defend against the threat this second Trump Administration poses. Yes, we must acknowledge our lack of attention, our failure to exercise all of our precious rights and freedoms as well as our sacred, necessary responsibilities as citizens. Finally, we would be both wise and more effective to take full responsibility for the presence of the conditions within our country that have contributed to the precipitous loss of human decency, compassion, and our connection to the wisdom of our hearts.

These are the very same things that have allowed some of our previous administrations to act in ways that have indeed "blurred decency and kindness, cheapened human life, and bred ill will and suspicion." And, this is the same combination of inaction and inattention, that have contributed to laying the foundation for the blatant lawlessness that was on display during the first Trump administration, that we continued to allow over the next four years at Mar-a-Lago and that is now being acted out in Washington by a President and his minions who appear to be willing to even defy the judicial rulings made by members of the co-equal Judicial Branch of government who have begun to order the President to cease his illegal encroachment on rights of Congress and the rights of We the People.

And this, unfortunately, could not be a clearer demonstration of precisely what Thomas Jefferson warned us about so long ago when he said,

> *"Once the people become inattentive*
> *to the public affairs*
> *you and I and Congress and Assemblies,*
> *Judges and Governors,*
> *(and I now add) and Presidents*
> *Shall all become wolves."*

So I have included Hoffer's words in this opening chapter to remind myself and I hope you as well, that if we fail to admit our flaws and deficiencies that have slowly corrupted our values and weakened our nation over time, and if we fail to support our courts in enforcing their decisions, and also fail to demand that Congress do its job, as a co-equal branch of government, we may never again be able to speak with true integrity, decency, courage, and strength of character. We will also fail to retake the high ground, the place from which we can successfully chart a course through these troubled waters.

The Gift of Being An American

I also believe that one of the most powerful tools We the People have at our disposal in our effort to defend our democracy and our way of life is gratitude - gratitude for being on this earth at this very propitious time and for having both the privilege and opportunity to do this important work of saving democracy and contributing to the well-being of humanity. We also have the opportunity to give thanks for the gift our participation in this quite extraordinary country during this pivotal stage of its experiment in collective governance provides. It is this experiment, built on a level of diversity and inclusion rarely experienced in human history, plus the unique promise it offers of liberty, justice, and the pursuit of happiness for all, that has provided us with an invaluable training ground on which to learn the right and just essentials needed to conduct this necessary defense at this time. Indeed, without this experience, I believe we, like so many of our brothers and sisters in countries around the world who have never had these rights and freedoms and this opportunity, would succumb mutely and subserviently, in this time, to the few wishing to control the many.

So, I pray with all of my heart that we will capitalize on these gifts, take advantage of our experience, and find the will and the courage to reconnect with the fundamental truths on which this nation was founded. I also pray we will forgive ourselves for our complicity in the sins our nation committed in the past. And that we will reconnect with the knowledge that it is these experiences that now allow us to recognize the true scope and danger of this current threat and the need to act decisively and quickly to defeat it.

Indeed, without our previous culpability, we would also not be able to reach out to these individuals who are lost and invite and encourage them to wake up from the hypnotic state they currently appear to be in and rejoin the true family of man before it is too late. We must also remember that these individuals who are now intent on our destruction are not an alien species but instead are simply angry, wounded human beings who have wandered off the path. They are frail and fractured brothers and sisters driven by a belief that they have been left out and left behind, something all of us have felt at various times.

But in the end, as disturbed, disillusioned, angry, and vengeful as they may be, and we need to do all that we must do to defend against their efforts to harm us, we would also be wise to take advantage of another piece of sound, common-sense from Eric Hoffer.

> **"You can discover what your enemy fears most,
> by observing the means he uses to frighten you"**.

So, let's take Hoffer's words to heart. Let's also stop chasing illusions and buying into the distractions that are currently being floated like trial autocratic balloons by this erratic and unstable President and his sycophants and instead follow the wisdom of our hearts rather than the noise that too often distorts our minds.

Let us also, as the wise and inspiring Mary Morrissey counsels us, listen to that still small voice within. Let us ask "the soul of our life and the god of our being, to help us to reconnect with our humility, honesty, compassion, and commitment to truth. These things and the practice of our unalienable rights and freedoms will allow us to not only successfully defend this imperfect, but still unique system of governance called representative democracy, but they will also help us find a way to successfully invite, at least some among those who are trying to destroy our way of life, back into the fold.

These qualities and characteristics can also help us to avoid falling victim to the same kind of anger, hate, violence, and the desire to exact revenge that this administration is currently exhibiting. It is sadly, a dark, dystopian premise to build a life upon. So, while defending our democracy, I invite us to do our best to see this President and his mimics for who they are, emotionally wounded and psychologically damaged. Yes, that beneath their dower, joyless demeanors, their callousness and blatant disregard for our well-being, and the evil they are attempting to rain down upon us, we would be wise to not treat them as the enemy, but instead as lost souls who are prisoners of their illusions, their limited beliefs, and their fears. And, as part of our defense against their efforts, let us be both clear and persistent in encouraging them to consult the wisdom of their hearts rather than relying exclusively on the false assumptions that distort their minds and, in this way, invite them to turn their ire and confusion into constructive contributions they can make to the family of man. In short, let us continue to encourage them to stop trying to break the world as some kind of distorted revenge for the emotional and psychological wounds that have, most likely, been visited upon them by members of their families and what can sometimes feel like a very unforgiving world.

While one cannot be sure they will be able to respond immediately, or in some cases at all, we can be certain that somewhere beneath the surface, these seeds of truth will be planted and that at some time, they will bear fruit for at least some of these disenchanted and distressed souls.

And this recommendation does not mean I believe we should turn a blind eye to the danger they pose. Instead,m that in defending against their efforts, we keep our hearts open and focus on the many remarkable and positive things we can do to support life on this challenged planet at this awkward time. For, as Buckminster Fuller has advised us and as I will do my best to help us remember as we take this journey:

> **"You never change things**
> **by fighting existing reality.**
> **To change something,**
> **build a new model**
> **that makes the existing**
> **model obsolete."**

Two Questions

I have also chosen to begin this book with this paraphrase of two questions posed long ago by the Jewish sage, Hillel the Elder –

CHAPTER TWO - FRAMING THE DILEMMA

"If not now, when? If not me, who?"

These words speak to me of other undeniable and essential truths that I believe we would be wise to keep in mind as we mount both our defense against those trying to destroy our form of government and our way of life and the strengthening of our democracy. One of these truths is that there is another path we can still take if we are honest, courageous, responsible, and responsive enough and if we act non-violently in a timely way. And this path begins with our answering Hillel's questions with a passionate, resounding "YES!"

If we do this. If we are each willing to make a major commitment to acknowledge and act on the fundamental truth that - We the People truly are democracy's best and last hope. If we couple this admission with the acceptance of our frailty and our accountability for the part we have played in the erosion of the foundation of core values and personal character that we identified above, and if we recognize that it is this erosion that has created the breeding ground for these lost souls and this current threat, we will surely find a way to rediscover the necessary strength, clarity, and renewal of genuine character to live the lives we were born to live.

The Invitation

So if you are a citizen of this democracy or someone hoping to become one; if you consider yourself to be a Republican or a Democrat, an Independent, a Libertarian, or perhaps someone who does not wish to declare any political affiliation at all, but you still care about the well-being of our way of life and the value of our unalienable rights, freedoms, and responsibilities; if you know in your heart that this new administration is not just out of alignment with who we are and what we stand for, but deeply and fundamentally opposed to both, and if you want to do your part in protecting our way of life even if you do not yet know how, then you are, as they say, on the right page at the right time and this invitation is meant for you.

For my part, I will do my best in these pages to honor your time and share what I believe is an accurate and true definition of the scope of threat we face, some of the actions that we failed to take in the past that could have prevented this Trump administration or anyone else from bringing us to this dangerous juncture. I will also do my best to offer some recommendations – in the form of the keys and cures – that I mentioned earlier and are drawn from history – our own and that of other nations - as well as from my own, first-hand experience consulting and coaching with some of the most notable corporations, government agencies, institutions, spiritual and religious organization and non-profits in the country, and the people who run them.

This experience has not only given me intimate looks into the belly of the beast but also allowed me the privilege of working with some extraordinary people who have demonstrated courage, integrity, and willingness in their efforts to change some of the elements and factors within their environments that contributed to these challenges. And I can say that it is this experience that gives me hope that as citizens, citizens in waiting, and as members of the Fifth Estate in this unique system of checks and balances that is one of the most valuable gifts given to us by our founders, we can, indeed, save our democracy.

There is one more thing I want to say before moving on. The more I consider the difference between the intrinsic concept of democracy, and the promise that it calls up in me, and the way it has been practiced, the more certain I am that the former is a lot more than a political practice. Instead, it is a sacred path that can allow humanity to arrive at a higher form of consciousness and to authentically continue its search for that "more perfect union, our founders identified.

I also realized this a year ago this week when I experienced a health crisis, the first in my 81+ years on this earth. It was, as so many things like this are, both a crisis and an opportunity.

During that experience, which included two weeks in Intensive care, I almost slipped over the edge on a few different occasions. That, of course, was the crisis. As for the opportunity, that came in the form of several lucid dreams that were remarkably instructive, and I was also gifted with the download of over 250 poems and song lyrics that speak not only to the challenges of our time but very specifically to the severity of the threat our democracy now faces.

As a result, the information I received served as an important personal wake-up call. It has allowed me to make a new commitment to spend less time in my head and more in my heart. To make a deeper commitment to stay present and do what I can to improve the quality of life in our time. These commitments have now also morphed into a new book titled The Great American Road Show and Anthem Song Book. And a new concept album called Democracy. The book will soon be out on Kindle and Amazon, and the album containing 20 of the lyrics from the book is now on SoundCloud (You'll find a link to it at the end of Chapter Eleven). It is my hope, that these songs will inform and inspire you and that they will soon become the soundtrack for a theatrical production or a live-stream special.

In the meantime, here are the lyrics from one of the songs in this concept album titled Democracy Three. It celebrates what I call democracy's sacred nature. So I will close this first chapter with these lyrics.

Democracy Three

Is not just a form of governance
We should protect
But the path toward higher consciousness
We can select.
Democracy is not
Just a way to deal
With challenges collectively

It's a way to demonstrate human responsibility
And qualities that mirror
Our higher aspirations.
Like cooperation and compassion
To name just two.
Like integrity, trust
And commitment to truth
To name another few.

I share these considerations
With you
Because without them it is clear
Humanity periodically
Devolves into insanity.
And if you doubt
My conclusion
Consult the Algonquin,
Cree & Ojibway
About Wetiko
A virus of the mind
They say.
And consult the good Dr. Carl Jung
About The Totalitarian Virus
The disease of the soul
That infected the Nazis
And that has so many
In our world today
In its relentless grip.

Democracy requires
Sensitivity, equality
And understanding
The opposite of

*Supremacy, dominance
And the denial of
Of equity.
It builds on the sufficiency.
Not fear of scarcity
Nor separation
Or aggression.*

*Yes democracy
Is much more than
Just a counterbalance
To autocracy.
It is a search for
Greater
Authenticity,
Humility
And unity.
It is a search for
Genuine humanity
Real Social justice
Opportunity and empowerment
For all
And sanity.
It's accountability
And responsibility
By each
For higher good
It's the willingness to surrender
To what is sacred
And to follow the path
To higher ground.*

*Democracy's
More than a political creed
My Friends,
It is the blueprint
for a level of future sanity.
The true evolution of humanity
And freedom and fulfillment
For the many
Not just for the few
And it is, my friends,
Very, very
Long overdue!*

Chapter Three - A Little Back Story

> *"What we reach for*
> *maybe different,*
> *but what makes us*
> *reach is the same."*
> –Mark Nepo

A Little Back Story

Before going more deeply into the threat, its potential consequences, as well as some of the keys and cures I believe can mitigate and defeat it, I am moved to tell you a little bit more about how I have come to be here on this page at this time and why. It is my hope this information will support you in better understanding some of the material that will follow and also confirm the truth found in the statement by my friend, the poet Mark Nepo, that begins this chapter.

I was born 82 and a half years ago in the second year of America's direct participation in WWII. It was another time of great threat, a time when the free world did not yet know if the Nazi scourge could be stopped.

I was born in a hospital in Cambridge Massachusetts, and raised for the first several years of my life in East Boston. So, in addition to being surrounded by the warmth and the nurturing of a large, extended Italian/American family, I, as a second-generation son of immigrants, was also, surrounded by monuments depicting historical aspects of America's beginning; I was also the recipient of a number stories about the Revolution. As a result, I can say that without being aware of it at the time, I was inducted into a very inspiring, and innocent experience of our country at a very young age.

The monuments included physical places, like Bunker Hill which was across the river from where we lived, and other places I visited with my family. Places with names like Concord, Beacon Hill, Salem, Boston Harbor, and the Boston Commons, all of which contained heroic statues, symbols, and other reminders of our nation's early history.

Then there were the stories I was told in school and at home about brave men like Samuel Adams, James Otis, and others who spoke at Faneuil Hall and encouraged independence from Great Britain.

Incidentally, when I was a young boy my father and mother owned and operated a grocery store in East Boston. Sometimes my father would take me on his weekly trip to downtown Boston to that very same Faneuil Hall. It had, at that time, been converted into a loud bustling wholesale meat, poultry, and produce marketplace that was manned by a small army of butchers in bloodied aprons and farmers and vendors in stained overalls and work boots who loudly touted their goods.

Although my father and others told me it was the same place I had learned about in school, the place that had once been viewed as "the cradle of our democracy," I must admit I had trouble picturing how that sprawling market with all of its disarray and tumult could be the same place I had seen depicted in drawings in my school books where those early, passionate champions had inspired others to march down to the harbor, board ships and throw bails of tea British tea into the water. And, in doing so, they had fired, what I was told, was the first salvo in the American Revolution.

My early memories also include a teacher reading The Declaration of Independence to my class when I was still quite young. I still remember being captured by words I did not fully understand, but that still somehow resonated deep inside me. Other things that were also part of my induction into democracy included the Pledge of Allegiance I recited in my class each morning. It gave me the feeling that I was, in my way, doing my part to honor that earlier time and those brave Americans. Then, there was the excitement and pride I often felt when I listened to the sounding of our National Anthem and the singing of America, The Beautiful. Perhaps those of you who are older had some of these experiences and felt some of these feelings as well when you were young.

These childhood experiences, of course, constituted a very biased introduction to our early history. So naturally, as I got older and started to learn different things, things not included in my initial introduction, my innocent concept of America took several direct hits. For example, the original depictions and stories I was first introduced to of those who were referred to at the time as Indians and the early settlers at Plymouth and in other colonies celebrating Thanksgiving were replaced by images of painted savages attacking wagon trains and slaughtering so-called innocent white people. Of course, what I did not find out until later was that our indigenous brothers and sisters were trying to defend their sacred lands we were stealing from them and that it was us, with our rifles and cannons, pitted against their bows and arrows, who were doing the majority of the slaughtering.

A little later, I learned from one of my history teachers who prided himself on telling us what he called "the real truth," that we also had a long history of breaking treaties with the indigenous people and eventually gave up all pretense of wanting to support them and instead banished them through atrocities like The Trail of Tears and other forced marches to the swamps of the South and the barren, lifeless deserts of the West.

Later still I learned that all of the romantic and sanitized images I'd been exposed to of Black people singing Old Man River and being seemingly content to smile and walk around saying, "Yes um, Master," were major distortions and misrepresentations depicted by white people trying to hide the sins of slavery and the inhumanity we had visited upon our black and brown brothers and sisters during their years of servitude and debasement. And these things, like so many other sins and hypocrisies we committed, were always justified - as are our sins that continue to this day - as necessary sacrifices to propitiate the God of Economics.

Through my sister, who was four years older than me, and my maternal grandmother, a remarkable old woman with a deep, quiet reservoir of strength and wisdom, I learned another truth. I learned that from the very beginning of our country, girls and women just like them, had been required to play an equal part in suffering the rigors of opening the frontier, facing the dangers posed by native American warriors, and of course, risking death in childbirth, something that occurred approximately 50% of time. But even with all of this, they were denied all other forms of equality, including the right to vote, to own property, or to have financial independence.

These were only a few of the things I learned that tarnished my innocent introduction to democracy, and as a result, I found myself with questions that I did not know how to answer or even who to ask. This was especially true with my parents who, like so many other first-generation immigrants, had lived through the Great Depression and the Second World War, and as a result, for them, America was a haven of safety and a country that could do no wrong.

As a result, for a long time, I lived with my confusion and with feelings of anger, betrayal, and even shame that these discoveries called up in me. And I found myself pulling further away from my early childhood fantasies about my country and into rebellion, something that would probably have continued indefinitely if Jack and Jackie Kennedy and the whole Camelot mystique hadn't come along.

I can't, of course, speak for you, but in that all-too-brief-time that they were on the world stage, I began to feel a renewal of pride and hope that some of the things I had once believed about my country were not illusions and deceptions, but instead actually signs that some of those noble goals might still be possible.

My interest in history in high school and college gave me additional insights into some of our country's actions and those of other countries around the world. I began to understand that we weren't alone in our sins. A few intellectually honest professors also reinforced this understanding. When I started traveling to other countries, my perspective on the US changed yet again.

It's not that I forgot about the things we had and, in some cases, still did that qualified us for inclusion on Eric Hoffer's list of evil governments, but I also began to better understand that we were not as bad as many other countries and I also found that some of my 'truth-telling' teachers and professors had not always told me the whole story either or at least, another version of it. For example, we had and were continuing to do some pretty heroic things in defense of freedom in places around the world, especially in support of our allies and others in need. Our nation was also built on diversity and a welcome that was extended to our shores to many different racial, ethnic, and religious people, something very few other countries did, and the vast majority do not do today.

There were also major struggles going on in our country to address our involvement in slavery and other repressions. Thanks to Jack and Bobbie Kennedy and Lyndon Johnson, real efforts were being made to right some of the wrongs of slavery and to provide people of color, as well as women and other minorities, some of their long-overdue rights. And, in truth, by comparison to some of the prejudices, class warfare, and other sins I encountered in other parts of the world, it seemed to me that somewhere in the American psyche some of those words and principles captured in The Declaration of Independence and our Constitution were still alive and struggling to make their mark. And that's when I admitted that in our imperfect world, I would probably have to acknowledge that we human beings were a strange and conflicted lot and there would most likely always be two parts to our story – the part that held the promise of democracy and that touched my heart and inspired me and the other part with all of the imperfect, unconscious and cruel daily practices that resulted in the some of the sins and hypocrisies that would most probably always trouble me.

Bringing Things Up To Date

So, as I sit here today, I am deeply grateful that I came to this understanding. It now allows me, even after having experienced so many of the other body blows to our democracy and my innocence that I have experienced over the years - including the assignations of both Kennedys, Martin Luther King, Malcolm X, and others, the ongoing civil rights struggles, the Vietnam War, Nixon, the false justifications for the tragic invasions of Afghanistan and Iraq, and now the unfolding of this current egregious threat by Trump and his rag-tag army of incompetents and obsequious revengers. Yes, even after all of these disappointments and confusions, I find that I am determined to keep searching for that other side of democracy that is the core component of the American dream. It is a precious and noble component that turns democracy, as I shared at the end of Chapter One, into much more than a political process. It is that path to a higher form of consciousness, not just for those in our country but for all of humanity. A path to an elevated way of living, an honoring of the other species and our precious habitat. It is a call that continues to pull at my heart and is, I believe, well worth answering.

This is what motivates the words that I am moved to write and prompts me to respond to the call that I believe is being sounded in the hearts of those of us who still believe in this extraordinary, unfulfilled promise of democracy. It is a call to those of us who are citizens of this country and to all of humanity to return to a truer and more constructive path, the path known as the Wisdom Tradition. And, it is this path that we can follow in pursuit of the promise hinted at in our Founding documents and so many of the great books and texts of the world.

This goal is clearly at odds with this current administration's callous indifference and its all-consuming quest for power, domination, and revenge. This more noble goal is also at odds with this administration's primary objective of subjugating the many to the rule of the few.

But, if we stay true to our commitment, this can become a story that We the People can focus on as we continue along toward creating a more perfect union and – and please notice the word 'more.' This word was selected to remind us that, on this human plane, true evolution is always a work in progress.

So, our initial focus needs to most definitely be on stopping this absurd desecration of our core values and this gross violation of the Rule of Law. Indeed, the actions of this current administration are violent, abusive, and akin to taking an ax to the platform on which we are all standing and wondering why the abyss below keeps getting closer to becoming our reality.

So let us honor this opportunity and save our democracy and then let us build on this base and strengthen the original values that launched this nation. Let us also begin the process of celebrating the next stage of our spiritual journey For these values and precepts are not only captured in our founding documents, as I said above, they are also found in the world's great books, have been advanced by all of the truly extraordinary spiritual and religious philosophies and have been demonstrated by wise teachers and guides who have walked this earth before us. And they will also be found if we will follow the wisdom of our hearts, recorded in the true DNA of being human.

For this reason, if we succeed in defending and strengthening our democracy, not only will We the People benefit now, but the generations that follow us will also benefit enormously. We will also give hope, promise, and courage to the millions of individuals who have only been able to view this experiment in democracy from afar. Our efforts will give them the courage to cast off their shackles and join us on this path. This, I believe, is the real reason autocratic and totalitarian leaders hate America so much and spend so much of their time trying to destroy us. They know intuitively that once their people witness our victory over this attempt to turn our democracy into some form of autocratic Kleptocracy, once they sense the power our rights and freedom contain, they know their days are numbered.

So, I am committed to defending this understanding, this noble promise, and this opportunity. And, I sincerely hope you are as well. For, when I look around at the world today, it becomes increasingly clear to me every day that time is running out, not only on our experiment in Representative Democracy but also for humanity and this extraordinary habitat that is struggling so mightily to sustain us.

So let those of us who are currently being challenged, recognize that this threat is a tremendous gift and a rare opportunity to make a fundamental choice. We can deny what is happening and, in this way, end up colluding with those intent on destroying our way of life and, with it humanity's hope for the future, or we can take the necessary, proactive, positive, and sacred steps to right the ship and change course before it is too late.

Chapter Four - Revisiting The Threat

> *Whatever the human condition may be neither an individual nor a nation can ever deliberately commit the least act of injustice without having to pay the penalty for it.*
> *-Henry David Thoreau*

The Threat

I must admit that as I make this commitment to myself and you to fully participate to the best of my ability in defending our democracy, I still find it hard to accept that Donald Trump was elected President for a second term. This man who, as our 45th President, launched The Big Lie which claimed that the 2020 Election had been stolen even though the results had been verified by all 50 states, the election was reported by Trump's security services as one of the most secure elections in history, and his Big Lie was rejected by more than 60 courts. It was, however the claim he had repeated over and over until he had managed to divide our nation. In the process, he also significantly increased people's distrust in our government and his malevolent effort to turn reality on its head. He then fomented a violent attack on Capital and a plot to prevent the certification of the 2020 election results and to obstruct the legal transfer of power to the duly elected 46th President.

During his time in office, he also colluded with our enemies, siding with Putin, cozying up to Victor Orbond, and praising other autocrats while doing his best to destroy our relationships with friends and allies. Unfortunately for all of us, he fumbled his response to the pandemic that, as of May 2, 2023, it is reported has resulted in the deaths of over 1.16 million Americans. And yet, even with all of this, he was still able to mislead enough of our well-meaning, but not very well-informed fellow citizens to retake the White House so he can now continue his obsessive quest to turn our democracy into an autocracy or something even more despicable.

As I say these words, I still find it all very hard to admit. But these facts and others go a long way toward confirming that there does appear to be what has been called a 'disease of the soul' that is having its way with a significant number of people in our country. And, this includes not only a substantial number of disaffected citizens but many elected and appointed officials. It also includes a significant number of people in other countries as well. I mean what else could account for the amount of irrational behavior, all of the chaos and disruption, and the regression to such extreme levels of conflict and aggression? And so, for this reason, I will do my best to share some of what I have learned about this "disease of the soul" in the next chapter. And, I trust you will find it of value.

For the moment, let me return to the identification of some of the crimes against We the People for which this man was scheduled to stand trial. He was charged in Florida with stealing and misusing top-secret documents. In Georgia with election interference. And in New York, he was charged and found guilty by two juries of his peers. One for falsifying documents and defrauding the people of New York of millions of dollars of tax revenue, and in another civil case he was convicted of physically assaulting a woman in a NY Department Store and then libeling her. And, had it not been for a very questionable ruling by the MAGA majority on the Supreme Court on Presidential Immunity, he would most certainly have been convicted in more of these cases and would, in all probability, have been barred from ever holding public office again.

But that did not happen, and so we and the world were witness to his lack of integrity and appalling ethics on full display on January 20, 2025, when he took the sacred oath of office to become the 47th President of the United States. And he did so in the same Rotunda of the Capital that he had caused to be attacked exactly one year before. I say lack of integrity and ethics because it was clear from all that he had said on the campaign trail and would say later in that very ceremony and on the days that followed that he had no intention of keeping the oath to protect and defend the Constitution. This was also made clear by the fact that he stood there with his hand above rather than resting on the bible. As I reflect on this image, I am reminded of a game some of us played as children. It was a game in which we sometimes crossed our fingers behind our backs while making a promise, believing if we did, that our promise wouldn't count. It is telling, I think, that as a so-called grown man who was taking an oath to become the leader of the free world, he would be capable of such an immature and superstitious act.

And yet, no matter what one calls it - unbelievable, absurd, or childish, the truth is that after running a dark and dystopian campaign based on a literal mountain of outright lies, distortions, and more disinformation than can ever be tabulated but certainly enough to divide the American people, trigger levels of hatred, threats of violence and increased fear of 'the other', he, with the collusion of the MAGA members of Congress and a segment of the media that pretended to be a purveyor of legitimate news, pulled off one of the greatest cons in history. And in this way, like a hungry fox, he has not taken possession of the keys to the hen house and unless he is restrained, none of us chickens are safe.

I believe nothing better demonstrates both the frailty and fickleness of human reasoning and the blindness that sometimes visits us all than this. And, of course, Hoffer had something to say about this as well when he described what occurred in Germany under Hitler –

> *"I can never forget that one of the most gifted,*
> *best-educated nations in the world, of its own*
> *freewill surrendered its fate into the hands*
> *of a maniac."*

So now, relatively early in this second Trump administration, he has already demonstrated his true colors, ill intentions, and very questionable judgments. And yet polls show that while his approval rating is lower at this time in his term than any other president in history and it continues to drop, many of the so-called MAGA faithful, and of course, his sycophants in Congress and on the Cabinet, at least in public, claim that all is well.

I believe that if these people had listened to his meaning rather than been distracted by his bluster and bluff during the campaign, they might now be able or willing to admit that a number of the things he promised were not empty threats or grandiose gestures, but instead dangerous things he actually would do, things that the vast majority of even those who voted for him did not vote for. But such admissions are not generally easily made by those of us who call ourselves humans, especially when we have been conned. And this is something we all have, at one time or another, experienced. This also confirms the cliche that suggests that the one thing we human beings fear the most, right below the fear of death on the list, is the fear of being wrong.

A Recap of Some of These Outrageous and Dangerous Things

While many of us are aware of some of the things that this man is currently doing to negatively impact our way of life and our democracy, things are happening so fast with our news and information services being so fragmented and so full of false narratives, I thought it might be a good idea to list just other atrocities our President has and continues to commit.

For those of you who are reading this and who are unaware of these facts, I hope you will benefit from them. And for those of you who are aware of many

CHAPTER FOUR - REVISITING THE THREAT

of them, I hope listing them in one place will give you even more reason to step into the heart of the defense of our way of life.

This list includes his promise to be a dictator on day one. And that is clearly what he has done. He has also given Elon Musk and his team of technology hackers and hustlers, none of whom are government employees or authorized by Congress, carte blanche to do what they are doing, which is to decimate all of our government agencies, fire what may end up being hundreds of thousands of Federal employees who perform essential services on behalf of We the People. And to add insult to injury, allowing this same team of hackers unauthorized access to many of the most carefully guarded databases that contain the most sensitive information on all citizens.

Then, of course, are his other dictator-like efforts to try to force Canada to become our 51st state, to forcefully acquire Greenland and the Panama Canal, and most troubling of all, his turn-about on Ukraine with his demand for a large percentage of their oil and precious mineral rights in return for further military aid. There is also his recent blaming of President Zalensky for the unprovoked war of aggression started by Russia. And, included in this atrocity is the President's lie about the amount the US has contributed to the war effort in Ukraine - an amount that was spent in the US to manufacture the weapons we supplied. And, on top of this, he insulted our NATO allies by undervaluing their contribution, which in point of fact, exceeded ours by over a billion dollars. And then, of course, the most egregious and dangerous act of all was to begin so-called Peace talks with Russia without consulting Ukraine, our NATO allies, or the members of Congress and then to report that he intended to remove all sanctions against Russia and to begin discussions regarding the formation of a new economic and political alliance with this outlier. These things are not only bizarre but constitute a gross overreach of authority on his part as well as a violation of our 70+ year NATO alliance and our commitment to Article V. which commits each NATO country including the U.S. to come to the defense of any country attacked by Russia or other bad actors. And, to top things off, this American President appears to be continuing his adoration of

Putin, even though only 2% of Americans polled support Putin and only 3% support Russia over Ukraine.

And there is so much more. Massive projected cuts to Medicaid which currently provides essential services to over 75 million Americans, particularly children and vulnerable elders, dramatic cuts to the workforce at the Veteran's Administration, and equally disastrous cuts to key research and medical services that support veterans. The announced illegal attempt to close the Department of Education, the elimination of all environmental programs at the EPA, the attempt to close US AID, - one of the most valuable programs our nation supports, the shutting down of all cyber security programs that protect us against Russia and other foreign actors, the firing of all members of the Joint Chiefs of Staff, and replacing them with far less qualified Trump loyalists, the attempt to declare all transgender people unfit for military duty, the scrubbing from the roles the names and bios of all female and people of color who surved our nation and are buried at Arlington Cemetary., the attempt to defund and shutter of all sections of the US Global Media Programs - including Radio Free Europe, Asia, Africa, etc, massive cuts in manpower and budget at the Social Security Administration and the closing of a number of its field offices and the redution of its phone services that could require between 75,000 and 85,000 older and disable people to file claims in person at these greatly reduced by number of offices when prior to these cuts appointments to file claims in person were already taking a month or more to make. Also of particular concern, are Donald Trump's efforts, with the collusion of the new Attorney General, to turn the Department of Justice into his instrument of revenge against people he claims are his enemies when in fact, they are individuals who either have simply been performing their duty to protect and enforce the rule of law or have run against him in election campaigns.

What is particularly troubling is that the majority of these actions are against the law and in violation of the Constitution and, I believe, demonstrate that this man truly believes he is not accountable to the people of this country and can, therefore. Do whatever he pleases regardless of the chaos and destabilizing impact these things may have on our country and the world at large Nor does he appear at all bothered by supporting rogue nations' who are violating the international Rule of Law, nor does he show any sense of accountability whatsoever to the people of this nation for our reputation as a trustworthy partner and a force for good and peace in the world. Indeed, these actions by this President demonstrate a truly dangerous and lawless man of questionable character and stability who is not only in violation of his oath of office but is unable to acknowledge that he was elected to the Office of President as a public servant and not the ruler of the world.

And, to compound these things, there are also his efforts to strip colleges and universities of their core responsibility to provide an opportunity for the expression of the right to freedom of speech, and exposure to the real facts of history rather than some sanitized White National story. The same applies to major institutions and museums regarding their displays, exhibits, and courses. Indeed, revenge, barely disguised disdain, and a large dose of hate seem to be his primary motivators. And the objects of his rage include the special prosecutors and their teams who did their job by trying to hold him accountable under the Rule of Law for the crimes he committed. The members of the free press whose courageous efforts allowed millions of us to track and learn about his crimes and his illegal schemes, and residents of this country who have the right to freedom of speech which he, through an arcane war-time law, has ordered his gutless Secretary of State to deny.

So contrary to this President's constant insistence that all of his actions committed during his first term were not crimes, but were only attempts by the Democrats to damage him politically, the real truth is that all of the charges against him were brought after thorough investigations by the Justice Department and the FBI and careful deliberations by Grand Juries and, in some cases, findings by juries of his peers.

So my request to all Americans is this. If you do not believe the facts I have presented, simply close your eyes when this man speaks, listen to him with your heart, not just your mind.

And for good measure, here are more items from the list of this man's crimes and misdemeanors. He is also seeking to exact revenge on those he also calls his enemies who just happen to be some of the most talented and highly credentialed people who worked with him during his first administration – cabinet secretaries, chiefs of staff, White House Counsels, generals, scientists, diplomats, and other key staff advisors. Many of these individuals came forward during the 2024 election to plead with us not to allow him anywhere near the White House ever again.

I could go on with the list: Appointing people to his cabinet who are unfit, unqualified, and blatantly opposed to the mission of the departments and agencies they are being tasked to run, destabilizing the Department of Health and Human Services by eliminating key research programs and appointing RFK, an unstable man, disowned by his family and desperate to spread his unproven theories on the gullible and the desperate, firing all independent Inspector Generals, defunding and trying to abolish independent financial oversight agencies, putting the Defense Department in the hands of a former Fox weekend show host who is a self-acknowledged alcoholic and seriously unqualified for the job.

Truly, even a casual reflection discloses that his man is not suited to be the President of the United States; he is an impostor whose only aim is to visit as much punishment and destruction on our nation and the world as possible. And yes, as I said earlier, unfortunately, a sufficient number of our fellow citizens, aided and abetted by what I believe is still to be uncovered voter fraud, have given this angry and vindictive fox the keys to the hen house.

One other thing that he is promoting that should, in the minds and hearts of We the People, support my contention that he has lost his mind and most certainly his heart, and this is his preposterous scheme for Gaza.

Yes, this self-proclaimed genius recently proposed a plan for Gaza that he claimed had the support of many world leaders. In reality, of course, his scheme has raised almost universal criticism, especially among leaders of Muslim countries and also concerned experts experienced in global issues and diplomacy from around the world. It is a plan, however, that his faithful mimics in Congress and a number who appear on what is truly 'fake news' are declaring is wonderful and innovative.

Thankfully, however, the rest of the world sees his plan for what it is, one of most egregious attempts at ethnic cleansing in history, as well as a poorly disguised power grab by the US for the Palestinian Homeland, an even more poorly disguised plan to support the far-right government in Israel to eliminate any chance of having a Two State Solution. It also constitutes one of the most ludicrous and preposterous real estate development concepts in history, one that only a fraudulent and failed real estate developer could envision. Indeed, with a straight face, this man has had both the audacity and the gross insensitivity to call it a plan to create The Gaza Riviera. Which, of course, is just what 2 million poor, starving, and displaced Palestinians savaged by war most need.

And, of course, as all of this confusion and tumult is being rolled out, the miracles he promised, even the minor ones like reducing the cost of eggs and groceries, have all taken a back seat to his ludicrous and dangerous schemes that now have his full attention. And, these include his obsession with tariffs that he wants to put on goods coming from the countries in the world that trade with the US, an action he tried and failed badly at implementing in his first term. And what is amazing is that even his former aids and advisors admit that no matter how many times he has been told that tariffs are not a means of generating income for our national coffers, but instead only a means of adding to the cost of basic goods American businesses and consumers must pay, a step that will surely result in high inflation that will certainly damage our current economy - he, like all men of limited intellect with substantial egos insists on proving the adage that the real definition of insanity is doing the same thing over and over in the same way and expecting a different result.

These things and his illegal attempt by Executive Order to alter the 14th Amendment and eliminate naturalized citizenship for children born in America of immigrant parents; his decision to withdraw from the Paris Accord at a time when climate change is devastating much of the world, and to withdraw as well from the World Health Organization at a time when new and possible pandemics are on the rise; his threats to end FEMA and deny federal aid to hundreds of thousands of Americans who have had their lives disrupted and the homes and towns destroyed by fires in California, and the last devastating hurricane in North Carolina, as well as his efforts to get Congress to pass a law giving him a third term in office and another to have his face carved on then the side of Mount Rushmore. Truly this man, unfortunately for himself and all of humanity has a very tentative grasp on both decency and reality and it is them man who also happens to be followed night and day by another man who has the nuclear codes for world destruction in the briefcase he carries that only the President can order or counterman.

In Extremis

These and other almost impossible-to-accept but fully verifiable truths have, I believe, catapulted our nation into a period not only of great confusion, shock, economic uncertainty, and danger but into a condition known as "In Extremis."

I borrow the term from nautical language that describes the situation in which the captain and crew of a ship in danger of collision, capsizing, or running aground, are instructed to abandon the traditional Rules of the Road normally followed by ships at sea and instead focus their combined skills, courage, imagination, creativity and out-of-the-box thinking to do everything and anything necessary and as soon as is humanly possible to save the ship. And this, my fellow Americans, is the very advice I believe with all my heart that We the People should follow at this time.

The Ship Called America

There is, therefore, no doubt in my mind and heart that the Ship called America is in imminent danger, and unless We the People, like and crew of a ship deemed to be In Extremis, shake off our confusion, shock, and disbelief that is increasing exponentially daily as the new administration shows its true colors, and, launch a very committed and effective resistance non-violently but using all of our unalienable rights, we run the risk of colluding in our demise.

These are just some of the reasons I believe We the People, cannot wait for a future election that, I pray with all my heart will produce the outcome we want. However, based on the strange and dangerous things this President is doing, I fear that if we do not resist him with all of our passion and commitment now in this early portion of his administration, we may not see a legitimate election in the foreseeable future. I believe therefore, that we must make a stand en masse now by using our God-given rights and privileges as citizens of these United States and by creating a common front with all activist, advocacy, legal champions, labor unions, and elected leaders who still value our democracy and our way of life. And I will have more to say about all of us in Chapter Five.

When I say all of our rights, freedoms, privileges, and responsibilities – I mean from our freedom of speech to our right to strike and. from our ability to peacefully protest to our right to conduct work slowdowns, boycotts, rolling general strikes, and what may also be necessary – a temporary tax withholding revol. After all, if Trump and Musk think they can attack our government structure with a chainsaw and greatly reduce and. in many cases, eliminate effective services and support We the People require, then it seems to me that we should take careful stock of exactly what we are taxes are paying for. Surely this administration cannot expect We the People, who often pay a far greater percentage of our earnings than the vast majority of our corporations and most assuredly than the 1% of our population that controls over 90% of the wealth in this country.

This is the reason I refer to the exercise of our rights, freedoms, and responsibilities as 'democracy's best and last hope.' And I pray this will become more and more obvious to more and more of us who call ourselves citizens as the level of disregard and lawlessness displayed by this administration continues.

Yes. We the People truly are not only the best and last hope, but the critical moral and ethical bulwark required to protect the spirit and essence of America. We the People are also the only hope there is to pass on to future generations the extraordinary promise of "life, liberty, and the pursuit of happiness." Indeed, we are the only ones who can ensure that other precious and essential things will survive including - our freedom from the arbitrary and capricious whim of dictators, our freedom to practice whatever religion or spiritual discipline we choose, and our freedom to work toward creating a more perfect union, which remains one of the dreams on which our nation was founded

In short, this is why I believe We the People are now being called to step forward to defeat this threat against our democracy and then take the most important next step of identifying some of democracy's apparent weaknesses and strengthening them.

Chapter Five- The Disease of The Soul

> *"Nothing doth more hurt in a state*
> *then that cunning men pass for wise."*
> - Francis Bacon

The Disease Of The Soul

As promised in the last chapter, before identifying a number of the essential and valuable things, I believe We the People can do to defend our democracy and our way of life, I want to spend a little time exploring what I referred to earlier as the debilitating "disease of the soul and virus of the mind" that appears to have a number of our leaders here in this country and around the world, and sizable minorities of citizens here in the U.S. and in other countries in its grip.

I was introduced to this psycho/spiritual affliction through the work of Paul Levy, a Jungian scholar whose book *Dispelling Wetiko* proved to be *a* real eye-opener for me. As a result of Paul's comprehensive work, I discovered that long ago, our indigenous brothers and sisters in the Algonquin, Cree, and Ojibwa tribes had identified this "disease of the soul" and called it **Wetiko**. I also learned that more recently, CG Jung in his study of the Nazi scourge, identified this same affliction and called it **"The Totalitarian Virus."**

Both definitions suggest that periodically in the annals of history when individuals, tribes, and even whole societies have failed to do the essential work of acknowledging and healing their individual and collective emotional and psychological wounds and unacknowledge tendencies that we currently refer to collectively as "our shadow" – this "disease of the soul" and "virus of the mind," that lies dormant in the psyches of all beings, is triggered and becomes active in human consciousness.

According to our Indigenous brothers and sisters, as well as to Carl Jung and other contemporary experts and authors who have studied this phenomenon, if left untreated, this "disease of the soul" and "virus of the mind," like other major diseases eventually spreads and sometimes takes over greater and greater portions of the psyche. In some cases, like cancer and other biological diseases, it eventually incapacitates the host.

In the case of this psycho-spiritual virus called Wetiko or The Totalitarian Virus, this taking control generally results in the afflicted individuals doing more and more things that become increasingly more irrational and destructive, first to others and eventually to themselves as well. A particularly unusual aspect of this "disease of the soul," is that, unlike other biological diseases that eventually demand the host's full attention because the effects are playing themselves out in the host's body, Wetiko is often first projected by the host onto others who are then viewed by the host as enemies. The afflicted host then attributes to others the wounds, frailties, flaws, and dangerous motives they possess. This leads, of course, to the demonetization of the other, and when things get really out of hand, as they eventually do, the afflicted create justifications to injure and, in some cases, to annihilate their projected enemy. This pattern has been demonstrated throughout history and most recently by the Nazi regime under Hitler and the Stalin regime in Russia with the persecution and slaughter of millions of Jews.

I admit this is a somewhat awkward and overly simplified explanation of how Wetiko and The Totalitarian Virus work. I hope, however, that it is enough to encourage you to look around at what is happening in the world today, especially in countries where authoritarianism is either already fully ensconced or on the rise - as is the case here in this country. I also hope this brief exposure to Wetiko and The Totalitarian Virus will encourage you to take your own deeper dive so that you can better recognize if and where this sad and troubling scenario is being acted and what some of the cures are that can be implemented.

For you see, instead of doing the healthy and rational thing of acknowledging their illness and seeking help to find a cure, those afflicted with Wetiko, and I certainly include Donald Trump and his MAGA faithful in this category, are projecting their wounds and their flaws, as well as their discomforts and their negative intentions onto the "other," which at this moment in time includes many of us, who they frame as their political enemies, as well as those who have been trying to hold them accountable – like the special prosecutors, other legislators, and members of the free press. They also project their fears and personal wounds onto the people they consider inferior and least able to defend themselves. Again, in this case, they call them immigrants or aliens. In short, they are people who are different because of the color of their skin, or because they have different cultural and ethnic backgrounds, different religious beliefs, and sexual orientations. In short, they are people who they believe are the easiest and most immediately available to demonize. The only thing I can say about this is - the payoff for those afflicted with Wetiko is going to be a real bitch.

It should also be clear that doesn't take Sherlock Holmes to recognize this tragedy that is now unfolding. All we need to do is open our eyes and acknowledge what we see. Open our ears and admit what we hear. And above all, open our hearts and feel what is true. Yes, instead of allowing ourselves to be misled by those afflicted with the awful realities of Wetiko and The Totalitarian Virus, we can let our love, compassion, and the wisdom of the heart lead us.

Although I have tried and, in some ways still do, to find another explanation for what is occurring in our world today, I have not been able to do so. Nor can I suggest a better way for We the People to address the condition of In Extremis we currently find ourselves in than by addressing the threat of Wetiko and The Totalitarian Virus,

So my recommendation is that we start today to do a much better job of addressing our shadows and that we do all in our power to encourage the MAGA Republicans and the White Christian Nationalists to also begin working on theirs. Both of these gifts will serve the well-being of the world.

So if you are not already familiar with *Wetiko* and *The Totalitarian Virus*, and you truly are committed to saving democracy and our way of life, I strongly encourage you to take the time to learn more about this "disease of the soul" and "virus of the mind" that is currently spreading across our nation and many other places on the planet for yourself. And I sincerely believe it will not only greatly benefit each of us that do, but our loved ones, future generations, and the world itself.

Cures For Wetiko & Keys To Saving Democracy

Just as Eric Hoffer's opening quote identified characteristics that contribute to a government being defined as evil, and that the first step in overcoming this evil is for We the People to admit our culpability and then be willing to change our behaviors and beliefs and demonstrate more enlightened and conscious acting and thinking, the same is true regarding the cure for Wetiko and The Totalitarian Virus. We must first admit to having a shadow side and then begin the essential work of healing the emotional and/or psychological wounds that cause our anger, hatred, cruelty, lack of compassion, and desire to dominate and destroy others.

In an earlier manuscript, The Power of One, I outlined a series of immediate and short-term, as well as medium and long-term keys or cures to save our democracy. Now, as I write these words, I am aware that these same keys and cures are precisely what can also help us address the "disease of the soul" that is destroying our nation and our planet.

This will help us regain our sovereignty and practice our unalienable rights and freedoms more fully, all of which are just and lawful. They will also help us regain our sanity and be much more inclined to grant all others their unalienable rights and freedoms, recognize our interdependence, and allow us all to remember that advancing the greater good of each individual is the only way to ensure the greater good for all of humanity. And I am confident that on the day we acknowledge this truth, we will have a genuine chance of creating a more positive future and of not only defending our democracy but strengthening it.

Other Keys and Cures

Expressing our creativity is another way to cure this "disease of the soul" and defend against the attempt to destroy our way of life. It is this understanding that can also give us a clue as to why the Trump Administration and its sycophants and supporters have come up with this nonsense and subterfuge about WOKE and now DEI. I believe what they are doing, whether consciously or not, is defending against their fear of expressing their creativity, which they, in all likelihood, intuitively sense will require them to acknowledge their affliction with Wetiko and The Totalitarian Virus and get on with the task of healing the wounds that drive them. This is one of the reasons they label us as liberals and "enemies of the state." I for one believe these MAGA Republicans intuitively sense that if they allow themselves to express their creativity, they will have to stop expressing the qualities and characteristics that Hoffer defines as evil.

Stop for just a moment and consider who these so-called "others " are that the MAGA mob criticizes. They are America's artists, writers, musicians, entertainers, positive visionaries, healers, innovators, and outstanding athletes. They are the people who bring us genuine breakthroughs in thought, physical levels of achievement, and new forms of expression that touch our hearts, inspire our minds, offer improvements and innovation in our systems and practices, as well as give us breakthroughs in science, medicine, and other healing modalities. They are our social and cultural innovators. They are our dreamers and adventures, who send their imaginations on flights out beyond the limited boundaries of our everyday world, and because of their efforts, they not only bring us joy and inspiration but also help us raise our consciousness, invite us to value our imaginations, support individual empowerment, practice of human rights and spread the gifts of freedom and our commitment to the greater good of the greatest number. If that's WOKE and DEI, then I say, "Brother, bring them on!"

It is also interesting that these so-called WOKE things, as you may note, are all things that those who are afflicted with Wetiko and The Totalitarian Virus fear the most because as Nelson Mandela so eloquently reminded us in his first inaugural speech.

> *"Our deepest fear is not that we are inadequate. Our deepest fear is that we are powerful beyond measure. It is our light, not our darkness, that most frightens us."*

Other cures for Wetiko are expressions of gratitude for all that we already have. Indeed, as our friend Lynn Twist, author of The Soul of Money, student of Buckminster Fuller, and founder of the Pachama Alliance, often says, "**What we appreciate, appreciates**."

Our compassion for others and ourselves, as well as our willingness to forgive ourselves and others, are both powerful cures for Wetiko and The Totalitarian Virus and powerful defenses against autocracy. Above all, our willingness to follow the wisdom of our hearts is a cure that will keep on giving no matter how it is expressed.

Each of these authentic and fundamental human expressions will allow us to begin to get a handle on this disease of soul and mind that has become so prevalent on our planet today. And if we begin to utilize even just the abbreviated list of cures and keys that you find in the next two chapters, as well as others offered by the great minds and hearts in our world, we can begin to take our next steps toward the birth of that long promised new level of human consciousness and, then from that higher vantage point, have the opportunity to continue our quest for a more perfect union.

For the sake of expediency at this critical time of In Extremis, I am choosing to only include 21 of the keys and cures that I believe are readily available to all of us and are the easiest to implement now to best heal ourselves and defend against this unprecedented condition of insanity that threatens our democracy and our way of life.

So please, whether you had enough of all of the turmoil and abuse and are ready to mount the barricades to defend our country or if you are trying desperately to run as fast and far away from what you intuitively sense is an upcoming confrontation as possible. Whether your goal is to keep your head down and hope that no one will notice you and therefore you will somehow be left unscathed by this rapidly evolving travesty, or if you find yourself somewhere else along this gamut from action to avoidance, I ask you to allow yourself to review the list of recommended actions in Chapter Six and Seven.

I also assure you that I have done my best to list only cures and keys that do not promote violence, division, separation, or hate. Instead, I believe these keys and cures can remind us that we are much more alike than we are different and that contrary to the long-claimed error made by those who have interpreted Darwin's work - as "the survival of the fittest" what Darwin and other astute observers of nature discovered is the value of cooperation and collaboration. And if We the People, take this ability to heart, I am confident that we can indeed regain our sovereignty, practice honor and integrity, seek truth, and express our genuine love and compassion for each other and all of humanity. And it will be these expressions and actions that will allow us to live the lives we were born to live, develop our skills, and share the talents, gifts, and promises we are here to contribute.

And one last thing. All of these cures and keys are ones that We the People are fully justified and entitled to practice. They are lawful, just, and honorable, provided we practice nonviolence. And there is some really good news is this. These expressions do not require a visa, a passport, the drafting of a new law or legislative action, a loan, or a financial investment. They do not even require a note from our mothers.

All we need to do is make a conscious choice to be better at being human. This is one of the reasons I stress nonviolence. Nonviolence is not only essential to the success of our individual and collective efforts during this time of challenge, but it will also prevent these malcontents who are committed to the destruction of our democracy from releasing the dogs of war against us. And, of even greater importance, nonviolence and a heartfelt expression of genuine love for our way of life and our rights and freedoms are the best paths we can take to save our nation and, ultimately, all of humanity.

If you doubt the veracity of this, take the time to learn a little more about the true nonviolent movements and the impact they have had on the history of the world. Jesus's recommendation to turn the other cheek gave birth to what continues to be one of the largest religions in the world. Buddhism speaks profoundly and has for centuries about the fact that none of us will get home until the least of us do. The foundation of the Quaker faith and the highest levels of Jewish, Sufi, Hindu, Chinese, and Tibetan mysticism all celebrate nonviolence.

And when I use this word, I do not mean its common connotation as a political tool. What I am talking about is nonviolence as a way of life that is infused in all of our thoughts, words, and actions. Indeed, it was this philosophy converted into action that caused a small, frail attorney who was forced off a train in India to one day lead his people to create a movement that forced the British Empire, the most powerful government in the world at that time, to leave India. And Gandhi and his followers did this without having to fire a shot.

Chapter Six - Creating A United Front

"There lies before us if we choose, continued progress in happiness, knowledge, and wisdom. Shall we choose death instead because we cannot forget our quarrels? Let us appeal, instead as human beings to human beings, Remember our humanity, and forget the rest."
Albert Einstein

Launching A National Campaign of Resolve

As I shared earlier, I believe that if We the People hope to be successful in defending against this attack on our democracy and also in addressing Wetiko and The Totalitarian Virus, we must each play our parts as citizens with urgency and great energy. And, we can only do this if we exercise all of our God-given rights and privileges and not just periodically when we go to the polls or when we have a few free minutes or it is convenient but as an essential component of what we do every day.

This effort will, however, be far more effective if we find a way to motivate and then collaborate with all of the activist, advocacy, and non-profit organizations that support the greater good, all labor unions that speak for the well-being of working people, all elected officials still in office or serving lifetime appointments as well as past elected officials including former members of Congress, the courts, current and past military leaders and members of the armed services, business, spiritual and religious leaders and their congregations who support our nation's best interests, experts and authors, leading scientists, healers, historians, professors and teachers, legitimate investigative journalists and conscious television news anchors, show hosts and many more of our best and finest minds and hearts who still believe in our form of government and our way of life and who are willing to act decisively, non-violently, and with true commitment, dedication, and persistence. As many teachers and guides who have walked these paths before us have told us, "**United we stand. Divided we fall**."

And, while forming this United Front may not be easy, especially when so many of the independent organizations and individuals mentioned above are deeply committed to their specific visions and missions, I believe it is essential to remind them that while their missions are valuable but without the umbrella of democracy the vast majority of their efforts will be made much more difficult, if not impossible, to execute. If you doubt the validity of my statement, I invite you to take a little time and discover how many voting rights, women's rights, freedom of speech, pro-environmental, social security and medicare advocacy, universal healthcare, minority or LGBTQ rights groups exist in autocracies and can execute their missions.

Indeed, as the attempted destruction of USAID that is thankfully still in question demonstrates, when there are hidden agendas at work and abuses of power by a man whose loyalty to our nation has been questioned repeatedly and whose head is filled with sugar plums – or perhaps in his case, with images of Big Macs and false fantasies of having unlimited power - We the People can be sure that it will take a truly united and committed front and a National Campaign of Resolve that issues a call to millions of Americans to come together in non-violent protest including work slow-downs, boycotts, and general strikes to dissuade this man and his obsequious minions from their dangerous, anti-American plans and actions.

Yes, I believe a United Front that can execute an aligned strategy that involves millions of Americans who are committed to defending Democracy in this time of In Extremis, is precisely what is needed. Otherwise, the Trump administration and its sycophants will execute their master plan that will remove any of the last remaining guardrails that still stand in the way of his becoming a dictator and our nation devolving into an autocracy.

And even if we succeed in forming a United Front, this will not be a cakewalk. For this man is so blinded by his quest for power and domination and his lust for riches at our expense, that he has lost touch with reality, and most assuredly with the role and duties of the Office to which he was elected. Indeed, he appears to believe that even though he was only elected by a rather slim margin - less than 1.5% of the people who voted - and the total number of people who voted for both candidates represents less than 2/3rds of the people who have the right to vote, it is clear that his claim that he received a mandate to implement the illegal things he's is doing is fraudulent. As is his inflated belief that he can do whatever he wants regardless of the needs and desires of even the people who voted for him, not to mention the millions of Americans who did not. All of whom are fully entitled to the support of this and all future administrations. Isn't that what our founders meant by 'One Nation Under God With Liberty and Justice For All'?

What is also important to remember is that this consummate manipulator ran for the presidency primarily in order to avoid having to deal with all of the major federal and state crimes he had already been or was about to be, indicted for. These were crimes that would have, in all likelihood resulted in prison sentences and, as a felon, his permanent disqualification from all future elected offices.

However, once his campaign began, he was introduced to this malignancy called Project 2025. He also began to be re-energized by the effectiveness of his lies and the physical frailty of Joe Biden. It was then that I believe Donald Trump's illusions and fantasies of ruling the world came back into full bloom, as did the scope and intensity of his deceptions and manipulations.

In retrospect, I can't help but think that this same man who raged for four years about others stealing the 2020 election from him and whose MO has always been to project onto others his maleficences, that this man and his allies somehow stole the 2024 election.

Couple this with the 'get out of jail' immunity card he received from the third tool in his autocrat's toolbox - the blatantly biased and co-opted MAGA majority on the Supreme Court, and it becomes very believable that the only person in a nation of over 330+ million people who was said to be above the law, broke the law to advance his malevolent purpose.

Masters Only In Their Fantasy Universe

Not even a bad writer of second-rate B-movie scripts would have the audacity to include these elements in one of them. And yet, currently running on the Washington Stage, one finds The Donald Trump Dog and Pony Show. A rather tawdry melodrama, I admit, but one in which he and his chorus of bad actors and mimics are trying to suggest they can run the most powerful nation in the world as if it is a small, mob-owned family business He also appears to believe - something that only a malignant narcissist could - that a man a who has managed to run a real mid-sized estate business with six major bankruptcies, a man who does not have the ability or propensity to read, to consult real experts and to recognize that he not only lacks the experience, but the intelligence to lead even the group of incompetents he has assembled, let alone lead a nation of over 330 million people that impact the more than 7 billion other people on this planet who are deeply interconnected and interdependent. Truly, only a deeply unconscious and troubled man could hold these illusions and not be bothered by the unmitigated tragedy that will surely result.

So the questions I believe We the People would be wise to answer – and I pray that we will do so quickly and with genuine passion and commitment – are these:

Are we clear that it is We the People and not this or any other administration or relatively small group of people, who are the reason this great country was created in the first place and for whom it now exists?

Are we clear that We the People are the lifeblood and soul of this nation and that it is our physical labor, energy, gifts and talents, dreams, aspirations, and financial support in the form of our taxes that make it possible for this nation to function? And that without We the People, this current administration or any other like it, as well as Congress, and the courts who in reality, and unfortunately for us, are composed primarily of a bunch of tired, old guys with limited intellects and even more limited imaginations who are holding on frantically to the illusion that they matter, when in reality without the full engagement of We the People, the majority of them couldn't change a tire, put in a light bulb or even find a fire exit?

Are we clear that we not only have all of the rights and privileges defined in our Declaration of Independence, our Constitution, our Bill of Rights, and a host of other laws that are on the books, but we also have the duty and obligation to use these rights every single day to ensure that those we elect as our public servants and employees do their job which is to represent our best interests and that we have the ultimate responsibility as citizens and members of the Fifth Estate o defend our nation against any all dangerous threats and condition we face, especially when our nation is experiencing a condition of In Extremist?

Chapter Seven - Eleven Individual Keys and Cures

*"I sit on a man's back, choking him
and making him carry me and yet assure
myself and others that I am very sorry
for him and wish to lighten his load by all
possible means - except getting off his back."*
- Leo Tolstoy

Eleven Individual Actions That Can Save Our Democracy.

What you will find in this chapter are eleven keys and cures that I believe We the People, can start utilizing today as individuals and then in concert with all of our advocacy and activist organizations, as well as those labor unions, legal defense organizations, elected and appointed officials who still believe in our democracy and our way of life, the constructive members of the free press, and conscious corporate, religious, and spiritual leaders, to get this administration to stop committing crimes, overreaching its authority, and trying to destroy our democracy.

These are eleven keys and cures we can each put to work in our daily lives to address some of the most dangerous and disturbing actions already being taken and others that are currently being planned by this abusive and illegal administration.

For example, at this moment in time, the administration is still announcing some cabinet appointments and submitting them to the Senate for approval. When one considers that the majority of these potential appointees are blatantly unfit and unqualified professionally for the jobs they are being advanced to fill, not to mention their lack of ethical and moral character and that their only real qualification is their willingness to execute this President lunacy rather than serve protect and defend our Constitution and the interests of the country, we must utilize one of our most precious freedoms – our right to Free Speech - to stop this travesty before it is too late.

Many of them, including Trump himself, also have obvious character flaws and they advance philosophies that rest on hate, violence, and revenge, things that make them a danger to our nation and humanity as well. So it is very important – no, it is critical to use our Freedom of Speech to flood the offices of the 53 MAGA Senators who ultimately get to decide whether to confirm them or not with texts, emails, phone calls, and office visits. The same thing holds for key aspects of the budget process, and to motivate these ethical sell-outs to get off their spreading deriers and start doing their jobs as a co-equal branch of government.

And know that a few hundred short communications will give them pause. A few thousand will help them remember they have an obligation to our country and not just to the man in the White House. And many thousands or hundreds of thousands of these communications from We the People can cause them to remember their oath of office and their commitment to do the things they were elected to do as well as the things their hearts and not their fears are telling them to do.

This same strategy should apply when actual bills are proposed in the House or Senate, especially bills that are abhorrent to We the People like cuts to Medicaid or Medicare or Social Security, or when a committee is formed to investigate people who do not require investigation – like the original January 6th Committee- or when the President issues an illegal Executive Order trying to change the 14th Amendment or when he arbitrarily decides has the right to negotiate an end to the war in Ukraine with Russia alone and without Ukraine and our NATO Allies at the table.

And this is just the beginning of these we must use our Freedom of speech to address. Signalgate is another example. When all of the major members of the security team, including the Vice President, the Secretary of State, the National Security Advisor, the Secretary of Defense, and others not only violate security protocols but then lie about it, hundreds of thousands, perhaps millions of us should be in the streets in Washington, silently, non-violently protesting and we should stay there until they all resign. This is the kind of power We the People have.

I also am not suggesting, of course, that each of us needs to do all of the things listed in this chapter and the next. But I am hoping that if we want to save our way of life then we and all of our activists, advocacy and non-profit organizations, our labor unions, former and current elected officials, members of legitimate news media, historians, and all who still believe in democracy will stop sitting on the sidelines like voyeurs or focusing on sub-issues and start doing our job as citizens.

And one more thing, before we get to some of the specific keys and cures I believe can help save our way of life. I believe the most important thing each of us can do, in this time of In Extremis, is to be sure we keep our hearts and minds open, stay committed to what is true and just, and remember that we are not dealing with enemies, just other human beings who have unfortunately lost their way.

I also believe we need to ask much more of ourselves, of those who lead us, and of society as a whole. It is clear that one of the major reasons we find ourselves in this truly dangerous place we find ourselves in today ay is that we have allowed the loss of personal character, the reduction in the practice of our core values, the degradation of our standards of behavior as individuals, and our inattention to civic engagement collectively to become acceptable.

And if there is any doubt about this, I remind you that our current President is a convicted felon, who owes hundreds of millions of dollars in fines for falsifying documents and using them to defraud the people of the state of New York. He is also, by his admission, a misogynist, and by his concepts and policies, a racist and homophobe. And, although he is currently doing all that he can to try to erase these and other facts from the public record, as I mentioned earlier, it is essential to remember he was found guilty in a civil case of physically assaulting a woman in a New York Department store and then libeling her. And yet, thanks to the support of a corrupt media organization that has almost single-handedly tried to eliminate truth from the airways, his approval rating among Republicans remains lower than most presidents at this stage of their term in office, but based on the facts listed above much too high.

So please hold this reality in mind as you review this list of keys and cures and decide how they can best serve you and our struggling nation.

1-Exercise Our Right To Free Speech. As citizens and members of the Fifth Estate it is essential and important to communicate our insights, recommendations, appreciation, and of particular importance, our objections and resistance and any possible solutions we believe can be applied to mitigate and defend against the policies, decisions, and actions already in motion or planned by the current Trump Administration, this Congress and The Supreme Court and in the future, against any next iterations of all three.

We the People would also be wise to recognize that this is not only one of our unalienable rights and freedoms but also one of our most important responsibilities. At least, this will need to be the case if we want to continue to have these rights and responsibilities and if we want to have a voice in determining what kind of country we want to live in and what kind of life we want to lead.

This advice applies equally to our interaction with our local, regional, and state elected officials, members of our state legislatures, and our local and regional courts.

And when I say this, I am not just referring to voting every two to four years or during special elections, attending an occasional town hall meeting, or making an occasional campaign donation. These are all good things in a representative democracy and in our efforts to elect good and faithful public servants. Unfortunately, however, when we are addressing the kind of threat we currently face, and are dealing with a dysfunctional political process that has been intentionally violated by elected officials with questionable ethical and moral standards, we need to play a much more committed role and demonstrate great honesty, truth, integrity, trust, and love.

We must recognize that the same rules and standards that apply in our best personal and professional relationships need to apply in our governance. At least, this will need to be the case if we want the kind of life we want and the kind of government that is necessary to support this kind of life.

To achieve this, we will have to prioritize our role as citizens more. We will need to invest more time and greater levels of cooperation, care, compassion, mutual respect, and love into our governing process. While this transformation is underway, it will be vital that we speak our truth often, in large numbers, and much more persistently in our interactions with the Trump Administration, this MAGA Congress, and the Supreme Court.

Although you may believe you are only one voice and that, as a result, you will not be heard, I assure you that you will be amazed at the impact even a relatively small number of communications in one or more formats— texts, emails, phone calls, office visits, and even petitions—will have on

Congressmen and Senators.

So if you add your outreach to those of even a handful of others and then hopefully to hundreds and then eventually to hundreds of thousands of others, you will discover how powerful your right to free speech is. All you have to do is do your best to make your message brief, your words truthful, speak from your heart, identify your concerns, and offer a possible solution if you have one. And, don't forget, you'll find all of the necessary contact information on the House, Senate, White House, Supreme Court, and other websites. You can also use Meta, X, Truth Social, TikTok, Blue Sky, and many other platforms.

Do this because if you, me, and our fellow citizens do not, the people in this administration, Congress, the courts, and as well as people in other countries who are wondering if Trump speaks for the American people, will make up whatever story suits their purpose about why We the People are silent.

Some Washington Access Information
  https://www.whitehouse.gov There is a contact form on this website
  Main Line - 202-456-1414. -Comments Line - 202-456-1111
  https://www.senate.gov.
  Alphabetical List of all Senators https://www.senate.gov/senators/
  Senators Are Listed Alphabetically On This Site
  All telephone extensions in the list of Senators should be preceded by 202-22
  https://www.house.gov/representatives/find-your-representative
  House Switch Board - (202) 224-3121
  The link above allows you to search by name for your representative
  The is no list on the House website of all representatives and their contact information
  For that list go to: https://clerk.house.gov/Members#MemberProfiles

2 - Exercise Our Right And Responsibility To Vote With Every Dollar We Spend Every Day.
Every day We the People, have many opportunities to vote with our dollars by spending them on products, services, and programs that

contribute to our physical, moral, and spiritual well-being, the well-being of other species, and our precious habitat.

If we do this and spend our dollars only in this way and with organizations that pay their fair share of taxes and are committed to the greater good and the well-being of their employees and contribute to the health of our planet. The same applies to programs and policies that are introduced by our governments at all levels.

If we do this, it will make a very significant difference in our world, especially when we consider that profit sits highest in the Pantheon of the Worshiped Gods by the vast majority of those committed to destroying our democracy.

We can also use our dollars to boycott products, programs, services, and especially candidates who do not support the greater good.

3-Remember that We the People Constitute the Fifth Estate, The Most Essential and Central Estate In Our Unique and Valuable System of Checks and Balances. While it is said that the Administration, Congress, and the Courts are three co-equal branches of government, and the Fourth Estate, the free press, should be the watchdog, it is We the People, The Fifth Estate that is the primary reason this nation was created and also the reason the other four estates even exist.

So, as members of the Fifth Estate, we would be both wise and much more effective if we exercised all of our unalienable rights and responsibilities. Not just some of them some of the time., but all of them as often as our hearts tell us to.

The more familiar we are with these rights and responsibilities and the more comfortable we get with exercising them, the faster they will become second nature, and we will use them effectively and powerfully as we go about our daily lives. Indeed, they will become as natural as our breathing and as valuable to our survival and to our ability to ensure that all of humanity has the chance to live the lives we were born to live.

4 -Always Honor and Exercise Our Right To Vote and Always Demand That Every Vote Be Counted. There is no excuse, barring some serious physical illness or disability, especially with vote-by-mail and early voting, for an individual not to vote and not to have their vote counted.

Failure to vote in two or more consecutive elections should involve inclusion on some kind of public list, and for those who continue this failure to exercise the vote, other privileges granted to citizens should be temporarily suspended until they either vote or demonstrate good cause for their failure to do so. Each of us who are citizens, without excuse or procrastination, should exercise the right to vote in every public election and whenever and wherever the opportunity to share our voice, our beliefs, and our recommendations. This includes our institutions, organizations, associations, businesses, clubs, churches, and even our family gatherings. It also behooves us to do everything in our power to ensure that we do not allow anyone, for any reason, to prevent anyone from exercising this right. And by doing this, we defend our rights and prevent tyranny from becoming a reality. In exercising our right to vote, it is also essential that we take the time to inform ourselves on the issues on the ballot and their real consequences and impact, and on the quality and character of those who stand for election. A nd to always vote after listening to the wisdom of our hearts rather than exclusively with the reasoning of our minds.

It is important to understand that at present approximately one million or more citizens who are entitled to vote currently do not participate in our national elections. So we would be wise to encourage everyone we know to vote and if they need a reason, ask them to look closely at what is happening in Washington today and to realize that this tragedy is taking place because of a difference in only 1 and ½ percentage points in the votes cast.

While there are individuals who are ill or incapacitated and may have real difficulties voting, there are many ways today that our citizens can exercise their rights, and much greater effort should be made to ensure that this number is greatly reduced.

We should also use the power of We the People to ensure that the Electoral College System is eliminated and that the popular vote determines who is elected President of These United States.

5-Exercise Our Right to Peaceful Assembly Including Sit-ins, Teach-ins, Work Slowdowns, Boycotts, General Strikes, and Temporary Tax Withholding Revolts. I believe we must use this cluster of our rights and freedoms now while it is still early in the tenure of this new administration and lawsuits are pending that dispute this president's violation of the law and attempted usurpation of Congressional authorities and when members of the free press are still very active in reporting the truth. I also believe we should be prepared to do this for as long as this administration is in office.

I also believe we should practice these rights and responsibilities not just in opposition to this administration but out of our love for our way of life, our freedoms, and this form of government that we know is not perfect, but is most definitely the path toward a much higher form of consciousness and the pursuit of the greater good for the greatest number than autocracy, theocracy, kleptocracy being advanced by this administration.

It is also essential that we are prepared to exercise this cluster of our rights that will have a substantial economic impact, for increasingly longer and longer periods until we not only get the full attention of this President and his sycophants in Congress and on the highest court but until our concerns are acknowledged and they begin to act on our requests.

This last recommendation is a very important part of our right to protest and it is the part that far too many of us fail to exercise. For example, although a remarkable number of Americans took part in the Woman's March after Trump's first inauguration, in The Black Lives Matter Movement after the killing of George Floyd, and many Americans are now thankfully beginning to protest many of the violations by the Trump administration, the truth is that protest marches that do not include utilize - work slowdowns, boycotts, and rolling general strike are far less successful than those that do.

Yes, protest marches make a lot of noise, draw a reasonable amount of attention to voter dissatisfaction and issues that need attention, and help individual citizens realize they are not alone in their concern unless a protest creates actual legislative reform, forces a reversal of a policy or action that is against the general well-fair, forces the firing of an individual or individuals who are abusing their positions or breaking the law or the resignation of an individual or individuals, and in extreme cases, the fall of an evil government, the protest has missed its mark.

So, it is my hope and prayer that we have the courage and persistence to continue exercising our right to protest and always include those elements that have an economic impact, that we always protest non-violently out of love for our rights and our way of life, and that we also do so until the job is done – even if this involves discomfort and sacrifice.

6 - Keep Our Eyes, Ears, Mind, and Heart Open and Acknowledge What Is Happening. As we have discussed, democracy is not a spectator support, but this doesn't mean it has to become a 24-hour-a-day obsession either. What this key means is that each of us needs to pay attention to what is going on, consult trusted and accurate sources of information to verify the truth of the position we are taking, and then do what our hearts tell us to do.

Yes, part of our responsibility as citizens is to stay informed and weigh in on those subjects that are important to us– on a local, regional, and national basis. And when we encounter something that our hearts tell us is out of alignment with the basic precepts, core values, policies, and practices defined and authorized by our Constitution, our Bill of Rights, and the spirit of our Declaration of Independence, we must speak up, ask questions, and not stop asking questions until we get honest and accurate answers from our public servants.

And as part of our protest, we should demand that our public servants reactivate the truth in advertising and communication laws and standards. And, above all doing all of these things we should keep two pieces of sage advice from Buckminster Fuller close at hand.

The first reminds us that.

> *"We are born to be the architects of the future and not its victims."*

And the second:

> *"You never change things*
> *by fighting the existing reality,*
> *To change something*
> *build a new model*
> *that makes the existing*
> *model obsolete."*

7.- Stop Responding and Reacting to the Opinions and Beliefs Held by Others. Instead, Act On What You know and Can Verify. It doesn't matter if the source of the information is a so-called expert or pundit or simply the usual and unavoidable local purveyor of gossip and innuendo. And most certainly, it doesn't matter if they are the President, a member of this or any other new administration, or one of the performing clowns and pretenders who masquerade as legitimate sources of the news and information.

Listen, if you choose to, but please listen with your heart and take the time to reflect, compare information from other trusted sources, and consider the implications before you act. In short, your job and responsibility as a citizen and a human being is to focus on what you know and not on what you or others believe. And, the best way to accomplish this is to always answer one simple and essential question. "IS IT TRUE?

Yes, if we want to live the lives we were born to live and if we want to preserve and protect the rights and freedoms we value most, we need to start living and acting on what we know based on our own experience, and that we measure in the sacred space of our hearts. If we do not know something, then we must demonstrate the courage to acknowledge this and be willing to continue asking questions and experimenting and testing until we get an answer that passes the heart test. Yes, we must take the time to do our research, compare perspectives, validate sources, and then test what learn. And then and only then we must do what we know to be right, do what is in our best interests, that of our families, and this nation. So stop taking 'wooden nickels' and chasing fool's gold. And always remember, if it sounds too good to be true, it generally is.

8- Stop Waiting and Hoping Someone Else Will Step Up And Do What Needs To Be Done. In short, take your cue from this old Chinese proverb. *"If everyone sweeps in front of their own house, eventually the whole street will be clean."* Do what you see needs doing. Not only will you feel empowered, but you will empower others and together you and they and all of us who comprise We the People will get a hell of a lot of remarkable things done.

9.- Remember That Democracy Is Not A Spectator Sport. Therefore, responsibility for its true health and stability does not rest exclusively in the hands of a President or the members of their Administration, nor with Congress nor with the Courts. And this is particularly true when it comes to this President and his sycophants, this new Congress, or the dysfunctional and out-of-control MAGA majority on the Supreme Court.

CHAPTER SEVEN - ELEVEN INDIVIDUAL KEYS AND CURES

Nor does our well-being rest primarily in the hands of those in our state capitals, legislatures, and city governments - particularly those who have also lost their way and who have been seduced and conned by this form of insanity known as the MAGA movement. And, although some members of the legitimate media have and continue to do a heroic job in trying to bring truth to We the People, we cannot depend solely on the courageous and trustworthy segment of the Fourth Estate alone to save us.

Instead, it is each of us who are citizens, residents, and citizens-in-waiting who must ultimately be responsible for the well-being of our democracy, the protection and preservation of the rights and privileges it affords us, and the extraordinary opportunities it offers us. Yes, it is We the People who are the primary reason democracy exists. This is why I believe Augustine of Hippo, known to most of us as Saint Augustine, suggested so long ago that,

> **"He who created us without our help,**
> **will not save us without our consent."**

So, in this time of "In Extremis," I believe with all my heart that We the People must reclaim our sovereignty. And although this may feel challenging, complicated, and, sometimes even beyond our reach; and while some of the things I have said may involve risk, especially to those of us who are accustomed to keeping our heads down, I assure you, playing it safe and pretending that "IT" could never happen here in this home of the proud and the brave, is a losing hand in a long term game that could last the rest of your life. For, as Helen Keller, who was without sight or hearing and yet lived a life of extraordinary accomplishments advised us,

> **"Life is either a daring adventure or nothing."**

We also cannot afford to be dissuaded from undertaking all of the other very real and necessary things we are responsible for doing, because those who are seeking to manipulate and control us offer false rationales or issue threats of punishment or violence. Nor should we be seduced by empty promises they will never fulfill, and most importantly, by our fears, concerns, or indifference.

Instead, like the crew and passengers on a ship that finds itself in a situation of In Extremis, we must use all of our skills, imagination, attention, energy, financial resources, and most especially, our courage, hope, and love of self, others, and country to do all that we can and must do to protect this hip called America from running aground, colliding with another nation or capsizing. We must exercise all of our unalienable rights and privileges, for they are God-Given and sacred. And we must use them not just occasionally when we vote or superficially when we have a little extra time. Instead, we must act boldly, always non-violently and persistently, and also remember the full implications and power of every one of our 'unalienable freedoms and rights.

10.- **Put the President, Vice President, and All Members of Congress On Notice That They Have Taken An Oath To Protect and Defend The Constitution and We Will Hold Them To It.** Many of us are relatively familiar with what occurs at the inauguration of an incoming president and vice president, but what all of us may not know is that the taking of the oath of office is not just a tradition; it is a Constitutional requirement for them to take their office.

US Constitution, Article II, Section 1 states, "Before he enters on the execution of his office, he shall take the following oath or affirmation:

"I do solemnly swear (or affirm) that I will faithfully execute the office of President of the United States, and will to the best of my ability, preserve, protect, and defend the Constitution of the United States. So Help Me God."

There is another oath that the vice president and every member of Congress, all justices on the Supreme Court, and many high-level appointees also take. It reads as follows:

"*I do solemnly swear (or affirm) that I will support and defend the Constitution of the United States against all enemies, foreign and domestic; that I will bear true faith and allegiance to the same; that I take this obligation freely, without any mental reservation or purpose of evasion; and that I will well and faithfully discharge the duties of the office on which I am about to enter: So help me God."*

Knowing this, it is our job as citizens and members of the Fifth Estate to not only remind them of their oaths of office but to hold them to them. And if they choose not to uphold their oaths it is our responsibility to use the full scope and power of our rights and freedoms to cause them to resign.

11 - **Read The Declaration of Independence, The US Constitution, and The Bill of Rights Periodically, Slowly, and Aloud.** Make it a point to read them with both your heart as well as your mind. These documents, as well as the wisdom in our hearts, contain all of the justification we or any future citizen of his nation require to justify using our rights and freedoms to defend and strengthen our way of life.

Please remember these are not just documents and words on paper, they represent a living trust created in blood by our founders and those who put their lives on the line for what they believed. And I believe they were divinely inspired and it is this inspiration that allowed them to pass on to us a foundation that if we continue refining and strengthening it, will lead us toward a state of higher consciousness and that more perfect union.

Remember democracy is not just a political process. Instead if you pay close attention to the rights, freedoms, and responsibilities identified in our founding documents, you will discover that democracy, and not autocracy, theocracy, kleptocracy, or corporatocracy with their repressions and denial of individual empowerment and sovereignty, is the only form of government that is a spiritual path. And it is this form of government that We the people have been entrusted with and that, if we have the courage and faith to defend it and the wit to strengthen it, will ultimately serve all of humanity.

For your convenience, you will find The Declaration of Independence in Chapter 11 and The Constitution and the Bill of Rights in the Afterword.

Chapter Eight - Ten Collective Keys and Cures

*"Don't be afraid to take a big step
if one is indicated.
You can't cross a chasm.
In two small jumps."*

-David Lloyd George

Ten Essential Collective Keys & Cures To Save & Strengthen Our Democracy

1-Form A United Front. To be successful in defending democracy, we need to do our part as individual citizens, but we also need to do what must be done in collaboration with our major advocacy and activist organizations, our most effective non-profits, our labor unions, and legal support organizations that support the greater good, the remaining champions of freedom and democracy who now are in the minority in Congress, the remaining members of the judiciary who still believe in the Rule of Law and all of the other elected leaders across the nation who still believe in the promise of our Republic, as well the remaining members of the media who are still fiercely and courageously attempting to report the truth.

In short, all of these organizations and individuals would be wise and a lot more effective if we agree to come together and form a united front with one and only one major goal – defending our democracy against every illegal and dangerous action, policy, piece of legislation or strategy this administration tries to execute.

And with the support of these organizations and individuals, We the People can more easily learn about and participate in major events, programs, and actions that will allow us to regain our sovereignty and then begin doing the things that are necessary to strengthen our democracy.

I realize in this age when the powers of the President have been continuously expanding to the point that many are now calling it The Imperial Presidency, this may seem like an impossible goal to accomplish, But I assure you, beneath all of the puffery and pontification, this President and his obsequious follower are bull and all bullies are ultimately afraid of having their bluff called. So, We the People should remind this President and his sycophants as well as others who will certainly come after him that they are our public servants and employees, and not our masters. And it is also essential to do this soon and every day during this administration until he and they get, the message, or are forced to resign.

We must also remind him and his obsequious mimics, that they have only one job to do, and that is to support our wishes and our well-being. And it should be clear having watched him strut around on the stage for these last 9 years, that the only way he will get this message is if we exercise our rights and responsibilities every day and in every way we can

When one considers the enormous number of systemic problems that threaten our survival as a species and the well-being of our habitat and the very brief time we have remaining to implement much-needed solutions, it would be nothing short of madness to believe we can accomplish this, as this President and his cronies suggest, by walking backward into the future clinging to a lot of limited beliefs, failed strategies and empty promises.

It will also be madness to fall for the absurd rouse that any one human being or even a small group of human beings have the wisdom, intelligence, and level of consciousness needed to best serve a nation of over 330 million people, who are interconnected with and interdependent upon the rest of humanity which now numbers above 7 billion. And if you believe that they can, all I can say to you is I have a bridge I want to sell you.

2 - Regain Our Oversight of the Administration, Congress, and The Courts. This does not mean we should not support our elected representatives, our courts, and the major institutions and organizations that contribute to the well-being of our nation. What it does mean, however, is that we should never allow our public servants and employees – and this includes our President, Vice President, all appointed officials, all members of Congress, and the Justices on the Supreme Court, complete autonomy or to allow them to either act or hold the belief once they are elected or appointed that they can do whatever they want, rather than doing their primary jobs which are defined by our Constitution and subsequent Amendments in our Bill of Rights and other laws passed by Congress, signed by the President and found to be legal by our Courts, that support the will of all of the people.

In short, we should support them only as long as they support the well-being of our democracy, honor their oaths of office, do not violate our rights, and demonstrate allegiance to advancing laws and programs that address our needs. But under no circumstances should the delegation of our rights be misconstrued by them as being permanent or absolute and this includes our delegation of authority to members of the Judiciary or others who are currently given lifetime appointments, a decision that should be changed by We the People at our earliest opportunity.

Lastly, it is absurd that all of the rules and policies that currently apply within the domains of the other three estates including those relating to the amount of salary they receive, the healthcare benefits they are entitled to, their retirement benefits, the amount of time they work, the number of days they are in session, the length of their vacations and time out of session and, most important, the bills, policies, agendas and issue they focus on, and the codes of ethic they are bound by, are determined by them. And yet they are our employees and public servants, so I believe we should reclaim and exercise our rights and responsibilities as members of the Fifth Estate and regain greater oversight and control over what they do and how they do it.

To this end, I believe that at least twice a year and always in person the President should deliver a true State of the Union Address - not the absurd nonsense currently being delivered which are little more than partisan political self-acknowledgment exercises. Instead, these State of the Union addresses should be realistic and accurate reports on what has been accomplished that is verified by facts rather than vague pontifications and bluster and also what has not yet been accomplished and how these two categories measure up to both the vision and mission announced at the start of their term or the beginning of the current year. Part of the report should also include obstacles encountered and suggested ways to resolve them, new agenda items, and more. In addition, paper reports should be published by the Office of the President monthly that track the progress between the two live, semi-annual State of the Union addresses.

Both Congress and The Supreme Court should also be required to deliver reports to We the People at the start of each annual session as well as periodically during each session. These reports should include a full plan of action and a clear vision statement, metrics and timelines, and self-evaluation of both successes and failures. And no new session of Congress or the Court should be allowed to begin, nor should any extended break be allowed to happen without a report to We the People on the progress made, things left undone or incomplete, recommendations offered and acted upon regarding both solutions and logjams. In short, our public servants and employees should report to We the People who they serve on how they are being responsible for our well-being.

3 - Ensure Term Limits And Ethical And Moral Standards Apply To All Elected And Appointed Officials. It is clear to many of us that many aspects of our system of government are dysfunctional and in need of significant refinement and repair. It is also clear that we should eliminate all lifetime appointments and that all governing bodies, courts, departments, and divisions of our government should operate under very clear and effective term limits and standards of behavior and ethics.

We also would be wise and put in place additional Parliamentary Procedures that give We the People the right to exercise Votes of Confidence so that any duly elected or appointed individuals, committees, etc., who fail to Protect and Defend the Constitution, violate the rules of ethics, fail to perform their functions and duties effectively, abuse their responsibilities or our rights and freedoms and fail to respond to our concerns when we express them, can be removed from their office or the bench at the time of their transgression by a Vote of No Confidence by We the People.

We should also exercise oversight over all elected officials and elected and appointed bodies on a regular basis. This means that We the People should have oversight and final approval of all of the elements listed in para 1. above.

Our public servants should, of course, participate in the structuring and formulation of these rules, policies, and organizational details, but ultimate approval of their decisions should reside with We the People and the process by which we approve these actions should continue to include periodic public votes, and also Votes of Confidence that can be called whenever a substantial number of We the People object or wish to revisit, refine, cancel or expand the decision reached by the individual or the body as a whole.

And if you wonder how We the People, who have stood on the sidelines for so long and much too silently, can get this done, remember the awesome power of peaceful assembly and non-violent protest, especially those that are combined with work-slowdowns, boycotts, and general strikes.

And if those in this new administration or any future administration do not want to agree to these changes – you guessed it – we should immediately conduct protests that are combined with sit-ins, teach-ins, work slow-downs, boycotts, general strikes, and tax withholding revolts for as long as necessary to convince them of the validity of our requests.

4- Reclaim Our Right to Determine How And On What Our Tax Dollars Are Spent. As you know, a significant amount of the funds used to run our government as well as funds that are spent on various programs come from our tax dollars or from funds authorized by Congress and advanced by the Treasury based on the assumption of what those tax revenues will be.

The problem, from the standpoint of effective government and We the People's oversight is that there is no control mechanism regarding the use of our tax dollars outside of the votes we cast for candidates for national public office every two to four years. So We the People currently have no way to truly exercise our control over how these tax funds are used.

I am, of course, aware that the Sixteenth Amendment authorizes our government to collect the taxes it imposes on all of us. I am also aware that there have, in the past, been many lawsuits contesting the legality of this amendment because of reported irregularities and disparities in the way it was ratified by some of the participating states. I am also aware that there was a ruling by the Supreme Court that prohibited further lawsuits.

However, in an age when the Supreme Court has chosen to override many long-held precedents and, in the case of the 2024 Presidential Immunity Ruling, simply make stuff up, it is clear that We the People should take it upon ourselves as the Fifth Estate to revisit the 16th Amendment and other primary tax laws.

In saying this, I am not suggesting that as citizens we should not be responsible for participating in supporting the financial stability of our nation. I do, however, believe, that this requirement becomes problematic when it is being administered by the current president and the brotherhood of billionaires, who somehow now believe they are no longer our servants, but our masters. It is also problematic primarily the President and not Congress, and We the People who is in control.

So in light of the current lawlessness being demonstrated by this President, We the People need to do whatever is necessary to take our seat at the decision table and have a much stronger voice in creating fair systems of taxation and financial support for our government.

In the meantime, I suggest that We the People create the kind of temporary tax withholding accounts with caveats attached that I have discussed in detail earlier in this book.

And if this administration or any other body is not willing to agree to this change – we exercise all of our rights of protest until they do.

5 - Keep A Close Eye On This Administration's Actions, Policies, and Programs. As difficult as it is to focus our attention on the many things this administration is doing in violation of the Constitution, our systems of checks and balances, and our rights, we must stay informed on what they are doing and, from a place of discernment and commitment, do what we can do today and every day to support the greater good. These are things we need to do to make it abundantly clear to those who are trying to destroy our democracy that we will resist them in every way possible.

At the same time, we would be wise to do all that we do with genuine love, compassion, integrity, trust, honor, courage, understanding, and support for our fellow Americans and our country. Unlike this President and members of his administration, we know that how we do things is as important as what we do.

6- Redefine The Election Process. This includes changing the length of elections, making it mandatory for all candidates to use public funds and only public funds, and to that end, we need to overturn all campaign finance laws that allow dark money to flow in unrestricted amounts into campaigns. We should also eliminate the Electoral College, increase requirements and qualifications for public service at all levels, reduce the length of service allowable, put very specific controls on campaign advertising, implement fact-checking of all candidates, with clear penalties, including expulsion from campaigns and elected office for those who are unwilling to comply.

Frankly, I find it incomprehensible that in a nation of over 330 + million people, we find ourselves electing so many partisan hacks and subservient water carriers who speak for special interest groups, for large funders who remain behind the scenes and have less than noble intentions.

It is also inconceivable and absurd that we often demand more preparation and instruction for those who want to qualify for standard technical certificates and operating permits for driver's licenses and tradesmen's permits than we do for those who run for public office, especially the Office of the President and also those who are given lifetime appointments to our courts or who are appointed to run our national, state and local agencies.

For this reason, I believe we should take a good and careful look at the requirements established for those who wish to lead us including and most especially those who seek to occupy the Presidency, and revisit and redefine these requirements as soon as possible.

When it comes to the role and responsibilities of our President, we should also question the assumption that any single individual who today serves as the Chief Executive of our nation of over 330 million Americans should have the same primary duties and powers as the Chief Executive of this nation when it was founded 248+ years ago when our population was estimated to have been approximately 2.5 million.

Those who wish to run for the highest office in the land, our Vice President, and all in the direct line of assuming the Presidency in times of emergency should also be required to undergo comprehensive background checks as well as take comprehensive emotional and psychological intelligence, and mental acuity tests before they can even announce their candidacy let alone occupying the office.

Individuals who wish to run for the highest office as well as for Congress, appointments to our courts, and all cabinet and other appointments should be required to take and make public comprehensive physical examines on at least an annual basis, and also be required by law to produce comprehensive financial, tax records. They should also be made to divest and show verification that while in office they have delegated all personal engagement in running private companies and organizations and controlling their investments. The Emoluments Clause for every individual elected to public office at the local, state, and federal levels should also be re-instituted and carefully and fully enforced.

And, as is the case with each of these recommendations, if We the People meet resistance in implementing these things we need to return our focus to the full exercise of all of our freedoms, rights, and responsibilities.

7 - Direct Our Attention To What Is Valuable, True, and Just. As responsible and engaged citizens we need to be discerning and responsible for what we read, where and how we get our news and information, what experts we listen to, and how we verify the truth and accuracy of what is being reported. In short, we should be informed, proactive, and responsible citizens.

When we encounter organizations, institutions, businesses, political candidates, business leaders, elected leaders, judges, and appointees who are not committed to the greater good and fulfilling their official duties, we should do all in our power first to put them on notice, and then, if they fail to adjust their practices, we should exercise our Vote of Confidence and force them to resign.

8- Commit to Maintaining Our Balance, Harmony and Healing. The world is too complex and the issues too important to place our faith in any one source, one person, or one belief system. It is true that as adults and as members of the Fifth Estate we have an important responsibility to learn the truth, test it, and apply it in the world for the greatest good of ourselves, our family and of the family of man.

Having read and reflected on the intent of our founding documents, another important thing I believe each of us can do as we go about our days is to utilize the many constructive means and tools that thankfully are at our disposal at this time in our history, including but not limited to: prayer and self-reflection, contemplation and mediation, various forms of therapy, experimentation with plant-based medicines, innovative breathing techniques, and many other constructive physical, emotional and psychological modalities to help us heal some of the personal wounds we all carry as well as contribute to the healing of some of our collective wound.

These practices will not only help stem the spread of the "disease of the soul" and "virus of the mind" known as Wetiko and The Totalitarian Virus that plague our time but these practices and modalities will help us realign our beliefs and actions with the truth in our hearts and with the guidance available to us through the Wisdom Traditions.

9 - Accept Short-term Discomfort And Sacrifice For Long-term Gain. To achieve our desired long-term goal of saving and strengthening our democracy, we must start today by using all of the tools at our disposal that we have discussed– emails, phone calls, and texts to people in elected office and the media. Letters to the editors, articles written for both print and internet circulation, podcasts, YouTubes, and TicTok posts that share the extent of our feelings and the scope and the level of our commitment.

We would also be wise to draft, circulate, and deliver petitions. And when I say petitions, I do not mean the fraudulent versions of petitions that have now become the political fundraisers' go-to tool. This disgusting practice of having citizens pay to express their insights and express their opinions is not only destroying our trust in political parties and our desire to share our opinions and beliefs, but it is also giving fund-raisers an easy way to avoid describing their missions and justifying their organization's need for our financial contributions.

We must also be willing to deal with some short-term inconveniences, including the sacrifice of some income, some comfort, and more. No truly effective strike was ever held that did not include these things. So let us have courage, discipline, and will to deal with short-term sacrifices to gain long-term, positive results.

10 - Create Personal Visions That Align With Our National Vision. We the People are encouraged to create both individual and collective visions that depict the future we want and the future we know humanity deserves.

We should create these visions from a place of love, compassion, understanding, and truth. We should do our best to include the specifics each of us wants to include as part of our reality including enough of all of our basic needs being met - and this applies to all of humanity- the ability to learn the essential lessons we have come here to learn; the ability to explore and develop our skills and talents and then the ability to share them for the greater good with others. The ability to express and share our love with everyone regardless of race, religion, ethnicity, and more. The ability to live in peace and harmony.

There are two pieces of advice that I suggest We the People remember in applying this key/cure. The first is from the author Somerset Maugham.

"It's a funny thing about life,
if you refuse to accept

anything but the best,
you very often get it."

This quote is from Lester Levenson, Founder of the Sedona Institute.

"Hold in your mind what you want
and only what you want and
that is what you will get."

Chapter Nine - Just A Few More Things

> *"Life is too short*
> *to be small."*
> – Benjamin Disraeli

Just A Few More Things

Having made this journey together, I ask, with all my heart, that all of us pay attention to the words included in this document from Eric Hoffer, Hillel, the Elder, Albert Einstein, Henry David Thoreau, Leo Tolstoy, Francis Bacon, Somerset Maugham, Lester Levenson, and those by Thomas Jefferson, Buckminster Fuller and Archibald MacLeish which I reproduce below.

> *"Once the people become inattentive*
> *to the public affairs,*
> *you and I and Congress and Assemblies,*
> *Judges and Governors,*
> *and Presidents*
> *Shall all become wolves."*
> –Thomas Jefferson

> We are born to be architects of the future
> and not its victims."
>
> –Buckminster Fuller

Heart/Head Coherence

I also invite you to take a few moments now and at regular intervals each day to close your eyes, take a few slow deep breaths, and re-establish the essential connection between your heart and your head.

Many of the wise ones who have gone before us have said that establishing this connection—what today is called Heart/Head Coherence—is one of the most valuable, challenging, and beneficial things each of us can do to transform the confusion, pain, and suffering in our world into greater consciousness, joy, individual empowerment, true abundance, compassion, and love.

A Daily Commitment

I also ask all of us to make a real commitment to do our job as proactive citizens every day in ways that are both small and large - like sharing your truth with a loved one, friend, or colleague, speaking out to an official in our government, our communities and to members of our families, when necessary participate in major protests that have real economic teeth. Do these things as part of your participation in your daily life, and it will never be said that when our democracy was seriously challenged, We the People were found wanting.

Pray Against The Odds

Lastly, I ask you to pray that this strange and unstable man and his rag-tag army of discontents realize there are choices they could be making other than those they are currently making. They could, for example, be deeply grateful and humble that they are being given a second opportunity to serve this nation, and instead of trying to destroy everything in sight, instead of focusing on settling petty grievances and seeking personal gain, they could be focused on the greater good.

They could also put their energy, effort, and talents to work, turning some of this nation's and the world's obvious flaws into strengths. They could cater not just to the needs of some of the people but they could serve the well-being of all of the people.

Instead of focusing on revenge, separation, and hate, they could focus on sharing genuine compassion, giving and receiving forgiveness, and expressing love for all of the people of this country and of the world. Instead of insisting on using others as objects of hate and violence, they could celebrate the sheer miracle and diversity of humanity. And, instead of trying to intimidate and cower both our allies and our so-called enemies, they imagine and then execute policies and practices, as leaders of the Free World, that would invite and encourage others to join them in addressing the truly systemic challenges of our time.

I know this no doubt feels like a long shot, but I believe that without taking our eye off the immediate challenge of defending our democracy and all of the rights, freedoms, and responsibilities we value, it is worth the effort to hold this vision that together – those of us on the left, the right, and in the center, and even those who do not know where they stand or for what – all of us on board what Marshal McLuhan called Space Ship Earth can come together and create a truly remarkable life on a truly miraculous earth.

And if we discover that change and genuine support from this President and his sycophants will not be possible, then let us put our shoulder to the wheel and use all of our rights. Freedoms and responsibilities as citizens and do all that is necessary to ensure that we limit the damage this strange and lonely man and his sycophants can do and also do what is necessary to drive them out of office and out of town as soon as possible.

The Saving Democracy Formula

Here's a summary of the formula I believe we can do to save democracy

- Make A Firm Commitment To Defend Democracy.
- Stay Awake.
- Keep Our Hearts and Minds Open.
- Practice Our Right To Free Speech Daily.
- Speak Our Truth On Things That Matter And To Those Who Need To Hear It.
- Use All Aspects of Our Right To Protest - March, Create Petitions, Conduct & Participate in Sit-ins, Teach-ins, Work-Slowdowns, Boycotts, General Strikes, and Tax Withholding Revolts, when necessary and for the greater good.
- Encourage Our Advocacy, Activist Organizations, Non-Profits, Current and Past Elected Officials, Labor Unions, All Religious, Spiritual & Fraternal Organizations, All Community Groups, etc. To Form A United Front and Support We The People In Saving Democracy
- Never Stop Exercising All Of Our Unalienable Rights and Freedoms, Not Even When We Think What We Are Trying To Achieve Has Been Accomplished.
- And Always Remember That Democracy And The Way of Life We Save Will Be Our Own.

I conclude this chapter with a quote from Archibald MacLeish that is as clear and valuable in its meaning to me as the quote by Eric Hoffer that opens this small book.

"There are those who will say that the liberation

*of humanity, the freedom of man
and mind is nothing but a dream.
They are right.
It is the American Dream.*

Chapter Ten - Next Steps & Special Bonuses

> *"You never change things*
> *By fighting existing reality.*
> *To change something, build*
> *A new model that makes*
> *The existing model obsolete.*
> -Buckminster Fuller

The Next Phase of The American Revolution!

Thank you for taking the time to read We the People, Democracy's Best & Last Hope. I hope you have found that some of the concepts and recommendations explored in these pages will support and inspire you during these awkward and challenging times.

I also hope they will encourage you to participate more fully and take greater accountability as a citizen for the well-being of our unique and valuable form of governance, our sovereignty, and our precious rights and freedoms.

As a citizen and member of the Fifth Estate, I trust these keys and cures will also support you in being vigilant and acting decisively, and always non-violently in addressing all challenges to our core principles and values, the Rule of Law and systems of checks and balances that have been the cornerstone of our democracy for 248+ years.

Above all, I hope you will always remember that We the People are the lifeblood and soul of America and the primary reason this nation was created. This, I believe, is why the Hopi Elders reminded us that **"We are the ones we've been waiting for."**

Also remember that when We the People demonstrate the will and courage to practice integrity, honesty, compassion, high ethical and moral values, trust, generosity, and always love and with a genuine commitment to the well-being of people not just here in America but everywhere, our democracy will be strengthened and our individual lives will be made even more joyful, sane and valuable.

I also ask us to remember to stay true to the best and most inspired aspects of our founding vision, to always be grateful and honor the extraordinary abundance of natural resources and the extraordinary beauty and abundance of natural resources this nation is blessed to have.

And I ask you to never forget that it is the sharing of our abundance, freedoms, and resources with people around the world that is not only our privilege but our responsibility to do so.

So I wish you well and trust you will take very good care of yourself and those you love, especially in these challenging times.

When time permits, I would love to hear from you and learn about your experience in practicing any or all of these keys and cures included on these pages and also some of your thoughts and recommendations about additional ways we can live the lives we were born to live and learn the lessons we have come here to learn. If you are inclined, I would also greatly appreciate your sharing a brief review of We the People - Democracy's Best and Last Hope on Amazon so that other potential readers will be encouraged to experience the benefits this book offers.

Here are some additional bonuses you can enjoy:

Visit The Ageless Living Series Site: https://www.agelesslivingseries.com/touchingtheheart. To watch our Telly Award Winning Two Hour Live Stream Special titled Touching the Heart and Dealing The Soul of America. It features over 100 musicians, dancers, singers, authors, experts, filmmakers, and ordinary Americans who celebrate Democracy and who contributed their talents and their wisdom to this special that seeks to close the divides and overcome some of the turmoil in our nation. It debuted one day before the 2020 Inauguration.

Go to Amazon Prime - Rent or purchase the Ageless Living Series our Award-Winning 40 Episode series at very affordable prices. The series features 22 popular Wisdom Keepers of our time sharing their inspiration and well-tested recommendations to support you in navigating the challenging waters of our time. You can also go to TUBI to see these programs with advertising included at no cost.

This link - https://www.agelesslivingseries.com/mymembership will give you to opportunity to join **The Wisdom Club**. This subscription will provide you with lifetime access, at one very affordable fee, to the work of some of the leading wisdom keepers of our time who performed live at a series of AgeNation Live Conferences in Santa Fe, on the Mile High Campus in Denver, in Chicago, in Seattle, and online. The Wisdom Club will soon offer the club members lifetime access to The Wisdom Library, an exclusive collection of interviews, podcasts, special programs, master classes, and more that are not available anywhere else.

Our weekly newsletter will provide you with inspirational quotes and tips for the road ahead and advance announcements on the release of new books like: Vol Two of We the People, The Great American Anthem Song Book, a collection of poems and lyrics on democracy (see below), and new individual and joint books by Sedena and me, some new master classes and even some special travel adventures.

Lastly, the concept album on Democracy that I recently created and discussed in several places in this book can be found at no cost on SoundCloud at this link below. **https://soundcloud.com/george-cappannelli/sets/the-great-american-anthem-road**

Until next time, I leave you with two things. First, these words are from French Cleric and Philosopher Pierre Teilhard de Chardin. They often help me, especially when I wander into some of my old and limited beliefs, to lift my line of sight and focus instead on why I am here and what I can do to contribute to the greater good. I hope his words will serve you as well.

> *"We are not human beings seeking a spiritual experience, but spiritual beings having a human experience."*

Second, the lyrics from one of the 20 songs in my new Democracy concept album. This one is titled:

All The World Was New

I dreamed that I awoke one day
And all the world was new
The divisions, the delusions and
Confusions spread
By a madman and a malicious few,
No longer blocked the sun
Or prevented anyone
From receiving their due.
And joy and friendship echoed
All across the land
And humanity
Was finally able to get back
to its intended plan

For the next stage revolution
Faster than evolution.
And in the heavens
The angels were singing
And on this fragile plain
The bells of freedom
And truth were ringing
I know it was only a dream,
my friends
But among the secrets in my heart
Is the knowledge that this dream
Can be our reality
If we can come together
Follow our hearts
And do our parts
I dreamed that I awoke one day
And all the world was new
Divisions and delusions and
The malevolence of the few
No longer blocked the sun
And everyone upon the earth
Received their due.

Much love and many blessings,
George

CHAPTER TEN - NEXT STEPS & SPECIAL BONUSES

Chapter Eleven - About The Author

> "The price of greatness
> is responsibility.
> -Winston Churchill

About the Author

George Cappannelli is an award-winning author, film and television producer/director, and sculptor, He has also served as a consultant and coach with a number of Fortune 500 companies, government agencies, and national associations, and has provided strategic coaching and innovative research in 3 Presidential Campaigns, a US Senate Campaign, and a local Mayoral Campaign.

He is the Co-Founder of AgeNation, a multi-platform media company dedicated to redefining what it means to live consciously and age wisely in the 21st Century. He is also the Co-Founder of Empower New Mexico, a 501C3 non-profit that serves the needs of elders.

In addition to his work in the corporate sector and his work on conscious living and wise aging under the banner of AgeNation, the company he co-founded with his wife, Sedena he has been privileged to work on projects with several world leaders including - Desmond Tutu, Lech Walesa, Golda Meir, Mother Teresa, and The Dalai Lama. As President and Founder of two New York film and television production companies, Theater Visions and Axial Productions, his work has been recognized with several International Film and Television Awards, as well as ANDY, CLEO, two special-category EMMY Awards, and Two Telly Awards. He served as Executive Director of The Sedona Institute and as one of the Members of The Society for the Advancement of Human Spirit, an organization chaired by The Dalai Lama.

He served as a lead facilitator for Insight Seminars and was a member of the group that supported the founding of The Insight Consulting Group. His background also includes work in the advertising and marketing field where he served as Executive Vice President and Creative Director of Allerton, Berman & Dean, A New York firm.

In 1991 he returned to the political arena where he managed a U.S. Senate Campaign in California. He also served as a strategic consultant in the 1992, 2000, and 2008 Presidential Campaigns. In 2004 served as the chief strategist in a mayoral campaign that elected the first Democrat in 30 years by the largest plurality in the town's history.

George Cappannelli is a well-known keynote speaker. His award-winning sculptures in stone, wood, and bronze are included in a number of public and private collections. As a writer, he is the co-author with his wife Sedena of Say Yes to Change, Authenticity, Do Not Go Quietly, The Best Is Yet To Be, and Getting Unstuck, and their new book Making The Best of The Rest of Your Life. (Due out soon.)

He is also the author of The Merlin Dialogues, It's About Time and Timelessness, A Man Is...a trilogy of novels entitled "Old Stones & Promises" and a new novel, Life After Life After...

He resides in Santa Fe with Sedena. She is the Co-founder of AgeNation and Empower New Mexico (a 501C2 organization) and co-producer and director of The Ageless Living PBS Television Series and of Touching The Heart and Healing The Soul, the Telly Awarding Winning Live Stream 2021 Pre-inaugural

Special.

Chapter Twelve - The Declaration of Independence

"Nearly all men can stand adversity
But if you want to test a man's character
Give him power."

-Abraham Lincoln

The Declaration of Independence.*

*Original Spelling and Grammer)

The unanimous Declaration of the thirteen United States of America, When in the Course of human events, it becomes necessary for one people to dissolve the political bands which have connected them with another, and to assume among the powers of the earth, the separate and equal station to which the Laws of Nature and of Nature's God entitle them, a decent respect to the opinions of mankind requires that they should declare the causes which impel them to the separation.

We hold these truths to be self-evident, that all men are created equal, that they are endowed by their Creator with certain unalienable Rights, that among these are Life, Liberty and the pursuit of Happiness. — That to secure these rights, Governments are instituted among Men, deriving their just powers from the consent of the governed, — That whenever any Form of Government becomes destructive of these ends, it is the Right of the People to alter or to abolish it, and to institute new Government, laying its foundation on such principles and organizing its powers in such form, as to them shall seem most likely to effect their Safety and Happiness. Prudence, indeed, will dictate that Governments long established should not be changed for light and transient causes; and accordingly all experience hath shewn, that mankind are more disposed to suffer, while evils are sufferable, than to right themselves by abolishing the forms to which they are accustomed. But when a long train of abuses and usurpations, pursuing invariably the same Object evinces a design to reduce them under absolute Despotism, it is their right, it is their duty, to throw off such Government, and to provide new Guards for their future security. — Such has been the patient sufferance of these Colonies; and such is now the necessity which constrains them to alter their former Systems of Government. The history of the present King of Great Britain is a history of repeated injuries and usurpations, all having in direct object the establishment of an absolute Tyranny over these States. To prove this, let Facts be submitted to a candid world.

He has refused his Assent to Laws, the most wholesome and necessary for the public good.

CHAPTER TWELVE - THE DECLARATION OF INDEPENDENCE

He has forbidden his Governors to pass Laws of immediate and pressing importance, unless suspended in their operation till his Assent should be obtained; and when so suspended, he has utterly neglected to attend to them.

He has refused to pass other Laws for the accommodation of large districts of people, unless those people would relinquish the right of Representation in the Legislature, a right inestimable to them and formidable to tyrants only.

He has called together legislative bodies at places unusual, uncomfortable, and distant from the depository of their public Records, for the sole purpose of fatiguing them into compliance with his measures.

He has dissolved Representative Houses repeatedly, for opposing with manly firmness his invasions on the rights of the people.

He has refused for a long time, after such dissolutions, to cause others to be elected; whereby the Legislative powers, incapable of Annihilation, have returned to the People at large for their exercise; the State remaining in the mean time exposed to all the dangers of invasion from without, and convulsions within.

He has endeavored to prevent the population of these States; for that purpose obstructing the Laws for Naturalization of Foreigners; refusing to pass others to encourage their migrations hither, and raising the conditions of new Appropriations of Lands.

He has obstructed the Administration of Justice, by refusing his Assent to Laws for establishing Judiciary powers.

He has made Judges dependent on his Will alone, for the tenure of their offices, and the amount and payment of their salaries.

He has erected a multitude of New Offices, and sent hither swarms of Officers to harass our people, and eat out their substance.

He has kept among us, in times of peace, Standing Armies without the Consent of our legislatures.

He has affected to render the Military independent of and superior to the Civil power.

He has combined with others to subject us to a jurisdiction foreign to our constitution, and unacknowledged by our laws; giving his Assent to their Acts of pretended Legislation:

For Quartering large bodies of armed troops among us:

For protecting them, by a mock Trial, from punishment for any Murders which they should commit on the Inhabitants of these States:

For cutting off our Trade with all parts of the world:

For imposing Taxes on us without our Consent:

For depriving us in many cases, of the benefits of Trial by Jury:

For transporting us beyond Seas to be tried for pretended offenses

For abolishing the free System of English Laws in a neighboring Province, establishing therein an Arbitrary government, and enlarging its Boundaries so as to render it at once an example and fit instrument for introducing the same absolute rule into these Colonies:

For taking away our Charters, abolishing our most valuable Laws, and altering fundamentally the Forms of our Governments:

For suspending our own Legislatures, and declaring themselves invested with power to legislate for us in all cases whatsoever.

He has abdicated Government here, by declaring us out of his Protection and waging War against us.

He has plundered our seas, ravaged our Coasts, burnt our towns, and destroyed the lives of our people.

He is at this time transporting large Armies of foreign Mercenaries to complete the works of death, desolation and tyranny, already begun with circumstances of Cruelty & perfidy scarcely paralleled in the most barbarous ages, and totally unworthy the Head of a civilized nation.

He has constrained our fellow Citizens taken Captive on the high Seas to bear Arms against their Country, to become the executioners of their friends and Brethren, or to fall themselves by their Hands.

He has excited domestic insurrections amongst us, and has endeavored to bring on the inhabitants of our frontiers, the merciless Indian Savages, whose known rule of warfare, is an undistinguished destruction of all ages, sexes and conditions.

In every stage of these Oppressions We have Petitioned for Redress in the most humble terms: Our repeated Petitions have been answered only by repeated injury. A Prince whose character is thus marked by every act which may define a Tyrant, is unfit to be the ruler of a free people.

CHAPTER TWELVE - THE DECLARATION OF INDEPENDENCE

Nor have We been wanting in attentions to our British brethren. We have warned them from time to time of attempts by their legislature to extend an unwarrantable jurisdiction over us. We have reminded them of the circumstances of our emigration and settlement here. We have appealed to their native justice and magnanimity, and we have conjured them by the ties of our common kindred to disavow these usurpations, which, would inevitably interrupt our connections and correspondence. They too have been deaf to the voice of justice and of consanguinity. We must, therefore, acquiesce in the necessity, which denounces our Separation, and hold them, as we hold the rest of mankind, Enemies in War, in Peace Friends.

We, therefore, the Representatives of the United States of America, in General Congress, Assembled, appealing to the Supreme Judge of the world for the rectitude of our intentions, do, in the Name, and by Authority of the good People of these Colonies, solemnly publish and declare, That these United Colonies are, and of Right ought to be Free and Independent States; that they are Absolved from all Allegiance to the British Crown, and that all political connection between them and the State of Great Britain, is and ought to be totally dissolved; and that as Free and Independent States, they have full Power to levy War, conclude Peace, contract Alliances, establish Commerce, and to do all other Acts and Things which Independent States may of right do. And for the support of this Declaration, with a firm reliance on the protection of divine Providence, we mutually pledge to each other our Lives, our Fortunes, and our sacred Honor.

I invite you to visit the Afterword. You'll find copies of the Constitution and Bill of Rights. there.

Afterword

The Constitution and The Bill of Rights

> "Security is mostly superstition. It does not occur in nature, nor do the children of man, as a whole, experience it. Avoiding danger is not safer in the long run than outright exposure. Life is either a daring adventure or nothing."

-Helen Keller

The Constitution of the United States: A Transcription

Note: The following text is a transcription of the Constitution as it was inscribed by Jacob Shallus on parchment (the document on display in the Rotunda at the National Archives Museum.) **The spelling and punctuation reflect the original.**

We the People of the United States, in Order to form a more perfect Union, establish Justice, insure domestic Tranquility, provide for the common defence, promote the general Welfare, and secure the Blessings of Liberty to ourselves and our Posterity, do ordain and establish this Constitution for the United States of America.
   Article. I.
   Section. 1.

All legislative Powers herein granted shall be vested in a Congress of the United States, which shall consist of a Senate and House of Representatives.

Section. 2.

The House of Representatives shall be composed of Members chosen every second Year by the People of the several States, and the Electors in each State shall have the Qualifications requisite for Electors of the most numerous Branch of the State Legislature.

No Person shall be a Representative who shall not have attained to the Age of twenty five Years, and been seven Years a Citizen of the United States, and who shall not, when elected, be an Inhabitant of that State in which he shall be chosen.

Representatives and direct Taxes shall be apportioned among the several States which may be included within this Union, according to their respective Numbers, which shall be determined by adding to the whole Number of free Persons, including those bound to Service for a Term of Years, and excluding Indians not taxed, three fifths of all other Persons. The actual Enumeration shall be made within three Years after the first Meeting of the Congress of the United States, and within every subsequent Term of ten Years, in such Manner as they shall by Law direct. The Number of Representatives shall not exceed one for every thirty Thousand, but each State shall have at Least one Representative; and until such enumeration shall be made, the State of New Hampshire shall be entitled to chuse three, Massachusetts eight, Rhode-Island and Providence Plantations one, Connecticut five, New-York six, New Jersey four, Pennsylvania eight, Delaware one, Maryland six, Virginia ten, North Carolina five, South Carolina five, and Georgia three.

When vacancies happen in the Representation from any State, the Executive Authority thereof shall issue Writs of Election to fill such Vacancies.

The House of Representatives shall chuse their Speaker and other Officers; and shall have the sole Power of Impeachment.

Section. 3.

The Senate of the United States shall be composed of two Senators from each State, chosen by the Legislature thereof, for six Years; and each Senator shall have one Vote.

Immediately after they shall be assembled in Consequence of the first Election, they shall be divided as equally as may be into three Classes. The Seats of the Senators of the first Class shall be vacated at the Expiration of the second Year, of the second Class at the Expiration of the fourth Year, and of the third Class at the Expiration of the sixth Year, so that one third may be chosen every second Year; and if Vacancies happen by Resignation, or otherwise, during the Recess of the Legislature of any State, the Executive thereof may make temporary Appointments until the next Meeting of the Legislature, which shall then fill such Vacancies.

No Person shall be a Senator who shall not have attained to the Age of thirty Years, and been nine Years a Citizen of the United States, and who shall not, when elected, be an Inhabitant of that State for which he shall be chosen.

The Vice President of the United States shall be President of the Senate, but shall have no Vote, unless they be equally divided.

The Senate shall chuse their other Officers, and also a President pro tempore, in the Absence of the Vice President, or when he shall exercise the Office of President of the United States.

The Senate shall have the sole Power to try all Impeachments. When sitting for that Purpose, they shall be on Oath or Affirmation. When the President of the United States is tried, the Chief Justice shall preside: And no Person shall be convicted without the Concurrence of two thirds of the Members present.

Judgment in Cases of Impeachment shall not extend further than to removal from Office, and disqualification to hold and enjoy any Office of honor, Trust or Profit under the United States: but the Party convicted shall nevertheless be liable and subject to Indictment, Trial, Judgment and Punishment, according to Law.

Section. 4.

The Times, Places and Manner of holding Elections for Senators and Representatives, shall be prescribed in each State by the Legislature thereof; but the Congress may at any time by Law make or alter such Regulations, except as to the Places of chusing Senators.

The Congress shall assemble at least once in every Year, and such Meeting shall be on the first Monday in December, unless they shall by Law appoint a different Day.

Section. 5.

Each House shall be the Judge of the Elections, Returns and Qualifications of its own Members, and a Majority of each shall constitute a Quorum to do Business; but a smaller Number may adjourn from day to day, and may be authorized to compel the Attendance of absent Members, in such Manner, and under such Penalties as each House may provide.

Each House may determine the Rules of its Proceedings, punish its Members for disorderly Behaviour, and, with the Concurrence of two thirds, expel a Member.

Each House shall keep a Journal of its Proceedings, and from time to time publish the same, excepting such Parts as may in their Judgment require Secrecy; and the Yeas and Nays of the Members of either House on any question shall, at the Desire of one fifth of those Present, be entered on the Journal.

Neither House, during the Session of Congress, shall, without the Consent of the other, adjourn for more than three days, nor to any other Place than that in which the two Houses shall be sitting.

Section. 6.

The Senators and Representatives shall receive a Compensation for their Services, to be ascertained by Law, and paid out of the Treasury of the United States. They shall in all Cases, except Treason, Felony and Breach of the Peace, be privileged from Arrest during their Attendance at the Session of their respective Houses, and in going to and returning from the same; and for any Speech or Debate in either House, they shall not be questioned in any other Place.

No Senator or Representative shall, during the Time for which he was elected, be appointed to any civil Office under the Authority of the United States, which shall have been created, or the Emoluments whereof shall have been encreased during such time; and no Person holding any Office under the United States, shall be a Member of either House during his Continuance in Office.

Section. 7.

All Bills for raising Revenue shall originate in the House of Representatives;

but the Senate may propose or concur with Amendments as on other Bills.

Every Bill which shall have passed the House of Representatives and the Senate, shall, before it become a Law, be presented to the President of the United States; If he approve he shall sign it, but if not he shall return it, with his Objections to that House in which it shall have originated, who shall enter the Objections at large on their Journal, and proceed to reconsider it. If after such Reconsideration two thirds of that House shall agree to pass the Bill, it shall be sent, together with the Objections, to the other House, by which it shall likewise be reconsidered, and if approved by two thirds of that House, it shall become a Law. But in all such Cases the Votes of both Houses shall be determined by yeas and Nays, and the Names of the Persons voting for and against the Bill shall be entered on the Journal of each House respectively. If any Bill shall not be returned by the President within ten Days (Sundays excepted) after it shall have been presented to him, the Same shall be a Law, in like Manner as if he had signed it, unless the Congress by their Adjournment prevent its Return, in which Case it shall not be a Law.

Every Order, Resolution, or Vote to which the Concurrence of the Senate and House of Representatives may be necessary (except on a question of Adjournment) shall be presented to the President of the United States; and before the Same shall take Effect, shall be approved by him, or being disapproved by him, shall be repassed by two thirds of the Senate and House of Representatives, according to the Rules and Limitations prescribed in the Case of a Bill.

Section. 8.

The Congress shall have Power To lay and collect Taxes, Duties, Imposts and Excises, to pay the Debts and provide for the common Defence and general Welfare of the United States; but all Duties, Imposts and Excises shall be uniform throughout the United States;

To borrow Money on the credit of the United States;

To regulate Commerce with foreign Nations, and among the several States, and with the Indian Tribes;

To establish an uniform Rule of Naturalization, and uniform Laws on the subject of Bankruptcies throughout the United States;

To coin Money, regulate the Value thereof, and of foreign Coin, and fix the Standard of Weights and Measures;

To provide for the Punishment of counterfeiting the Securities and current Coin of the United States;

To establish Post Offices and post Roads;

To promote the Progress of Science and useful Arts, by securing for limited Times to Authors and Inventors the exclusive Right to their respective Writings and Discoveries;

To constitute Tribunals inferior to the supreme Court;

To define and punish Piracies and Felonies committed on the high Seas, and Offences against the Law of Nations;

To declare War, grant Letters of Marque and Reprisal, and make Rules concerning Captures on Land and Water;

To raise and support Armies, but no Appropriation of Money to that Use shall be for a longer Term than two Years;

To provide and maintain a Navy;

To make Rules for the Government and Regulation of the land and naval Forces;

To provide for calling forth the Militia to execute the Laws of the Union, suppress Insurrections and repel Invasions;

To provide for organizing, arming, and disciplining, the Militia, and for governing such Part of them as may be employed in the Service of the United States, reserving to the States respectively, the Appointment of the Officers, and the Authority of training the Militia according to the discipline prescribed by Congress;

To exercise exclusive Legislation in all Cases whatsoever, over such District (not exceeding ten Miles square) as may, by Cession of particular States, and the Acceptance of Congress, become the Seat of the Government of the United States, and to exercise like Authority over all Places purchased by the Consent of the Legislature of the State in which the Same shall be, for the Erection of Forts, Magazines, Arsenals, dock-Yards, and other needful Buildings;—And

To make all Laws which shall be necessary and proper for carrying into Execution the foregoing Powers, and all other Powers vested by this Constitution in the Government of the United States, or in any Department or Officer thereof.

Section. 9.

The Migration or Importation of such Persons as any of the States now existing shall think proper to admit, shall not be prohibited by the Congress prior to the Year one thousand eight hundred and eight, but a Tax or duty may be imposed on such Importation, not exceeding ten dollars for each Person.

The Privilege of the Writ of Habeas Corpus shall not be suspended, unless when in Cases of Rebellion or Invasion the public Safety may require it.

No Bill of Attainder or ex post facto Law shall be passed.

No Capitation, or other direct, Tax shall be laid, unless in Proportion to the Census or enumeration herein before directed to be taken.

No Tax or Duty shall be laid on Articles exported from any State.

No Preference shall be given by any Regulation of Commerce or Revenue to the Ports of one State over those of another: nor shall Vessels bound to, or from, one State, be obliged to enter, clear, or pay Duties in another.

No Money shall be drawn from the Treasury, but in Consequence of Appropriations made by Law; and a regular Statement and Account of the Receipts and Expenditures of all public Money shall be published from time to time.

No Title of Nobility shall be granted by the United States: And no Person holding any Office of Profit or Trust under them, shall, without the Consent of the Congress, accept of any present, Emolument, Office, or Title, of any kind whatever, from any King, Prince, or foreign State.

Section. 10.

No State shall enter into any Treaty, Alliance, or Confederation; grant Letters of Marque and Reprisal; coin Money; emit Bills of Credit; make any Thing but gold and silver Coin a Tender in Payment of Debts; pass any Bill of Attainder, ex post facto Law, or Law impairing the Obligation of Contracts, or grant any Title of Nobility.

No State shall, without the Consent of the Congress, lay any Imposts or Duties on Imports or Exports, except what may be absolutely necessary for executing it's inspection Laws: and the net Produce of all Duties and Imposts, laid by any State on Imports or Exports, shall be for the Use of the Treasury of the United States; and all such Laws shall be subject to the Revision and Controul of the Congress.

No State shall, without the Consent of Congress, lay any Duty of Tonnage, keep Troops, or Ships of War in time of Peace, enter into any Agreement or Compact with another State, or with a foreign Power, or engage in War, unless actually invaded, or in such imminent Danger as will not admit of delay.

Article. II.
Section. 1.

The executive Power shall be vested in a President of the United States of America. He shall hold his Office during the Term of four Years, and, together with the Vice President, chosen for the same Term, be elected, as follows

Each State shall appoint, in such Manner as the Legislature thereof may direct, a Number of Electors, equal to the whole Number of Senators and Representatives to which the State may be entitled in the Congress: but no Senator or Representative, or Person holding an Office of Trust or Profit under the United States, shall be appointed an Elector.

The Electors shall meet in their respective States, and vote by Ballot for two Persons, of whom one at least shall not be an Inhabitant of the same State with themselves. And they shall make a List of all the Persons voted for, and of the Number of Votes for each; which List they shall sign and certify, and transmit sealed to the Seat of the Government of the United States, directed to the President of the Senate. The President of the Senate shall, in the Presence of the Senate and House of Representatives, open all the Certificates, and the Votes shall then be counted. The Person having the greatest Number of Votes shall be the President, if such Number be a Majority of the whole Number of Electors appointed; and if there be more than one who have such Majority, and have an equal Number of Votes, then the House of Representatives shall immediately chuse by Ballot one of them for President; and if no Person have a Majority, then from the five highest on the List the said House shall in like Manner chuse the President. But in chusing the President, the Votes shall be taken by States, the Representation from each State having one Vote; A quorum for this Purpose shall consist of a Member or Members from two thirds of the States, and a Majority of all the States shall be necessary to a Choice. In every Case, after the Choice of the President, the Person having the greatest Number of Votes of the Electors shall be the Vice President. But if there should remain two or more who have equal Votes, the Senate shall chuse from them by Ballot the Vice President.

The Congress may determine the Time of chusing the Electors, and the Day on which they shall give their Votes; which Day shall be the same throughout the United States.

No Person except a natural born Citizen, or a Citizen of the United States, at the time of the Adoption of this Constitution, shall be eligible to the Office of President; neither shall any Person be eligible to that Office who shall not have attained to the Age of thirty five Years, and been fourteen Years a Resident within the United States.

In Case of the Removal of the President from Office, or of his Death, Resignation, or Inability to discharge the Powers and Duties of the said Office, the Same shall devolve on the Vice President, and the Congress may by Law provide for the Case of Removal, Death, Resignation or Inability, both of the President and Vice President, declaring what Officer shall then act as President, and such Officer shall act accordingly, until the Disability be removed, or a President shall be elected.

The President shall, at stated Times, receive for his Services, a Compensation, which shall neither be encreased nor diminished during the Period for which he shall have been elected, and he shall not receive within that Period any other Emolument from the United States, or any of them.

Before he enter on the Execution of his Office, he shall take the following Oath or Affirmation:—"I do solemnly swear (or affirm) that I will faithfully execute the Office of President of the United States, and will to the best of my Ability, preserve, protect and defend the Constitution of the United States."

Section. 2.

The President shall be Commander in Chief of the Army and Navy of the United States, and of the Militia of the several States, when called into the actual Service of the United States; he may require the Opinion, in writing, of the principal Officer in each of the executive Departments, upon any Subject relating to the Duties of their respective Offices, and he shall have Power to grant Reprieves and Pardons for Offences against the United States, except in Cases of Impeachment.

He shall have Power, by and with the Advice and Consent of the Senate, to make Treaties, provided two thirds of the Senators present concur; and he shall nominate, and by and with the Advice and Consent of the Senate, shall appoint Ambassadors, other public Ministers and Consuls, Judges of the supreme Court, and all other Officers of the United States, whose Appointments are not herein otherwise provided for, and which shall be established by Law: but the Congress may by Law vest the Appointment of such inferior Officers, as they think proper, in the President alone, in the Courts of Law, or in the Heads of Departments.

The President shall have Power to fill up all Vacancies that may happen during the Recess of the Senate, by granting Commissions which shall expire at the End of their next Session.

Section. 3.

He shall from time to time give to the Congress Information of the State of the Union, and recommend to their Consideration such Measures as he shall judge necessary and expedient; he may, on extraordinary Occasions, convene both Houses, or either of them, and in Case of Disagreement between them, with Respect to the Time of Adjournment, he may adjourn them to such Time as he shall think proper; he shall receive Ambassadors and other public Ministers; he shall take Care that the Laws be faithfully executed, and shall Commission all the Officers of the United States.

Section. 4.

The President, Vice President and all civil Officers of the United States, shall be removed from Office on Impeachment for, and Conviction of, Treason, Bribery, or other high Crimes and Misdemeanors.

Article. III.

Section. 1.

The judicial Power of the United States, shall be vested in one supreme Court, and in such inferior Courts as the Congress may from time to time ordain and establish. The Judges, both of the supreme and inferior Courts, shall hold their Offices during good Behaviour, and shall, at stated Times, receive for their Services, a Compensation, which shall not be diminished during their Continuance in Office.

Section. 2.

The judicial Power shall extend to all Cases, in Law and Equity, arising under this Constitution, the Laws of the United States, and Treaties made, or which shall be made, under their Authority;—to all Cases affecting Ambassadors, other public Ministers and Consuls;—to all Cases of admiralty and maritime Jurisdiction;—to Controversies to which the United States shall be a Party;—to Controversies between two or more States;— between a State and Citizens of another State,—between Citizens of different States,—between Citizens of the same State claiming Lands under Grants of different States, and between a State, or the Citizens thereof, and foreign States, Citizens or Subjects.

In all Cases affecting Ambassadors, other public Ministers and Consuls, and those in which a State shall be Party, the supreme Court shall have original Jurisdiction. In all the other Cases before mentioned, the supreme Court shall have appellate Jurisdiction, both as to Law and Fact, with such Exceptions, and under such Regulations as the Congress shall make.

The Trial of all Crimes, except in Cases of Impeachment, shall be by Jury; and such Trial shall be held in the State where the said Crimes shall have been committed; but when not committed within any State, the Trial shall be at such Place or Places as the Congress may by Law have directed.

Section. 3.

Treason against the United States, shall consist only in levying War against them, or in adhering to their Enemies, giving them Aid and Comfort. No Person shall be convicted of Treason unless on the Testimony of two Witnesses to the same overt Act, or on Confession in open Court.

The Congress shall have Power to declare the Punishment of Treason, but no Attainder of Treason shall work Corruption of Blood, or Forfeiture except during the Life of the Person attainted.

Article. IV.

Section. 1.

Full Faith and Credit shall be given in each State to the public Acts, Records, and judicial Proceedings of every other State. And the Congress may by general Laws prescribe the Manner in which such Acts, Records and Proceedings shall be proved, and the Effect thereof.

Section. 2.

The Citizens of each State shall be entitled to all Privileges and Immunities of Citizens in the several States.

A Person charged in any State with Treason, Felony, or other Crime, who shall flee from Justice, and be found in another State, shall on Demand of the executive Authority of the State from which he fled, be delivered up, to be removed to the State having Jurisdiction of the Crime.

No Person held to Service or Labour in one State, under the Laws thereof, escaping into another, shall, in Consequence of any Law or Regulation therein, be discharged from such Service or Labour, but shall be delivered up on Claim of the Party to whom such Service or Labour may be due.

Section. 3.

New States may be admitted by the Congress into this Union; but no new State shall be formed or erected within the Jurisdiction of any other State; nor any State be formed by the Junction of two or more States, or Parts of States, without the Consent of the Legislatures of the States concerned as well as of the Congress.

The Congress shall have Power to dispose of and make all needful Rules and Regulations respecting the Territory or other Property belonging to the United States; and nothing in this Constitution shall be so construed as to Prejudice any Claims of the United States, or of any particular State.

Section. 4.

The United States shall guarantee to every State in this Union a Republican Form of Government, and shall protect each of them against Invasion; and on Application of the Legislature, or of the Executive (when the Legislature cannot be convened) against domestic Violence.

Article. V.

The Congress, whenever two thirds of both Houses shall deem it necessary, shall propose Amendments to this Constitution, or, on the Application of the Legislatures of two thirds of the several States, shall call a Convention for proposing Amendments, which, in either Case, shall be valid to all Intents and Purposes, as Part of this Constitution, when ratified by the Legislatures of three fourths of the several States, or by Conventions in three fourths thereof, as the one or the other Mode of Ratification may be proposed by the Congress; Provided that no Amendment which may be made prior to the Year One thousand eight hundred and eight shall in any Manner affect the first and fourth Clauses in the Ninth Section of the first Article; and that no State, without its Consent, shall be deprived of its equal Suffrage in the Senate.

Article. VI.

All Debts contracted and Engagements entered into, before the Adoption of this Constitution, shall be as valid against the United States under this Constitution, as under the Confederation.

This Constitution, and the Laws of the United States which shall be made in Pursuance thereof; and all Treaties made, or which shall be made, under the Authority of the United States, shall be the supreme Law of the Land; and the Judges in every State shall be bound thereby, any Thing in the Constitution or Laws of any State to the Contrary notwithstanding.

The Senators and Representatives before mentioned, and the Members of the several State Legislatures, and all executive and judicial Officers, both of the United States and of the several States, shall be bound by Oath or Affirmation, to support this Constitution; but no religious Test shall ever be required as a Qualification to any Office or public Trust under the United States.

Article. VII.

The Ratification of the Conventions of nine States, shall be sufficient for the Establishment of this Constitution between the States so ratifying the Same.

The Word, "the," being interlined between the seventh and eighth Lines of the first Page, The Word "Thirty" being partly written on an Erazure in the fifteenth Line of the first Page, The Words "is tried" being interlined between the thirty second and thirty third Lines of the first Page and the Word "the" being interlined between the forty third and forty fourth Lines of the second Page.

Attest William Jackson Secretary

done in Convention by the Unanimous Consent of the States present the Seventeenth Day of September in the Year of our Lord one thousand seven hundred and Eighty seven and of the Independance of the United States of America the Twelfth In witness whereof We have hereunto subscribed our Names,

The Bill of Rights: A Transcription

Note: The following text is a transcription of the enrolled original of the Joint Resolution of Congress proposing the Bill of Rights, which is on permanent display in the Rotunda at the National Archives Museum. **The spelling and punctuation reflect the original.**

On September 25, 1789, the First Congress of the United States proposed 12 amendments to the Constitution. The 1789 Joint Resolution of Congress proposing the amendments is on display in the Rotunda in the National Archives Museum. Ten of the proposed 12 amendments were ratified by three-fourths of the state legislatures on December 15, 1791. The ratified Articles (Articles 3–12) constitute the first 10 amendments of the Constitution, or the U.S. Bill of Rights. In 1992, 203 years after it was proposed, Article 2 was ratified as the 27th Amendment to the Constitution. Article 1 was never ratified.

Transcription of the 1789 Joint Resolution of Congress Proposing 12 Amendments to the U.S. Constitution

Congress of the United States begun and held at the City of New-York, on Wednesday the fourth of March, one thousand seven hundred and eighty nine.

THE Conventions of a number of the States, having at the time of their adopting the Constitution, expressed a desire, in order to prevent misconstruction or abuse of its powers, that further declaratory and restrictive clauses should be added: And as extending the ground of public confidence in the Government, will best ensure the beneficent ends of its institution.

RESOLVED by the Senate and House of Representatives of the United States of America, in Congress assembled, two thirds of both Houses concurring, that the following Articles be proposed to the Legislatures of the several States, as amendments to the Constitution of the United States, all, or any of which Articles, when ratified by three fourths of the said Legislatures, to be valid to all intents and purposes, as part of the said Constitution; viz.

ARTICLES in addition to, and Amendment of the Constitution of the United States of America, proposed by Congress, and ratified by the Legislatures of the several States, pursuant to the fifth Article of the original Constitution.

Article the first... After the first enumeration required by the first article of the Constitution, there shall be one Representative for every thirty thousand, until the number shall amount to one hundred, after which the proportion shall be so regulated by Congress, that there shall be not less than one hundred Representatives, nor less than one Representative for every forty thousand persons, until the number of Representatives shall amount to two hundred; after which the proportion shall be so regulated by Congress, that there shall not be less than two hundred Representatives, nor more than one Representative for every fifty thousand persons.

Article the second... No law, varying the compensation for the services of the Senators and Representatives, shall take effect, until an election of Representatives shall have intervened.

Article the third... Congress shall make no law respecting an establishment of religion, or prohibiting the free exercise thereof; or abridging the freedom of speech, or of the press; or the right of the people peaceably to assemble, and to petition the Government for a redress of grievances.

Article the fourth... A well regulated Militia, being necessary to the security of a free State, the right of the people to keep and bear Arms, shall not be infringed.

Article the fifth... No Soldier shall, in time of peace be quartered in any house, without the consent of the Owner, nor in time of war, but in a manner to be prescribed by law.

Article the sixth... The right of the people to be secure in their persons, houses, papers, and effects, against unreasonable searches and seizures, shall not be violated, and no Warrants shall issue, but upon probable cause, supported by Oath or affirmation, and particularly describing the place to be searched, and the persons or things to be seized.

Article the seventh... No person shall be held to answer for a capital, or otherwise infamous crime, unless on a presentment or indictment of a Grand Jury, except in cases arising in the land or naval forces, or in the Militia, when in actual service in time of War or public danger; nor shall any person be subject for the same offence to be twice put in jeopardy of life or limb; nor shall be compelled in any criminal case to be a witness against himself, nor be deprived of life, liberty, or property, without due process of law; nor shall private property be taken for public use, without just compensation.

Article the eighth... In all criminal prosecutions, the accused shall enjoy the right to a speedy and public trial, by an impartial jury of the State and district wherein the crime shall have been committed, which district shall have been previously ascertained by law, and to be informed of the nature and cause of the accusation; to be confronted with the witnesses against him; to have compulsory process for obtaining witnesses in his favor, and to have the Assistance of Counsel for his defence.

Article the ninth... In suits at common law, where the value in controversy shall exceed twenty dollars, the right of trial by jury shall be preserved, and no fact tried by a jury, shall be otherwise re-examined in any Court of the United States, than according to the rules of the common law.

Article the tenth... Excessive bail shall not be required, nor excessive fines imposed, nor cruel and unusual punishments inflicted.

Article the eleventh... The enumeration in the Constitution, of certain rights, shall not be construed to deny or disparage others retained by the people.

Article the twelfth... The powers not delegated to the United States by the Constitution, nor prohibited by it to the States, are reserved to the States respectively, or to the people.

ATTEST,

Frederick Augustus Muhlenberg, Speaker of the House of Representatives
John Adams, Vice-President of the United States, and President of the Senate
John Beckley, Clerk of the House of Representatives.
Sam. A Otis Secretary of the Senate

Constitutional Amendments 1-10 make up what is known as The Bill of Rights. Amendments 11-27 are listed below.

AMENDMENT XI

Passed by Congress March 4, 1794. Ratified February 7, 1795.

Note: Article III, section 2, of the Constitution was modified by amendment 11. The Judicial power of the United States shall not be construed to extend to any suit in law or equity, commenced or prosecuted against one of the United States by Citizens of another State, or by Citizens or Subjects of any Foreign State.

AMENDMENT XII

Passed by Congress December 9, 1803. Ratified June 15, 1804.

Note: A portion of Article II, section 1 of the Constitution was superseded by the 12th amendment. The Electors shall meet in their respective states and vote by ballot for President and Vice-President, one of whom, at least, shall not be an inhabitant of the same state with themselves; they shall name in their ballots the person voted for as President, and in distinct ballots the person voted for as Vice-President, and they shall make distinct lists of all persons voted for as President, and of all persons voted for as Vice-President, and of the number of votes for each, which lists they shall sign and certify, and transmit sealed to the seat of the government of the United States, directed to the President of the Senate; — the President of the Senate shall, in the presence of the Senate and House of Representatives, open all the certificates and the votes shall then be counted; — The person having the greatest number of votes for President, shall be the President, if such number be a majority of the whole number of Electors appointed; and if no person have such majority, then from the persons having the highest numbers not exceeding three on the list of those voted for as President, the House of Representatives shall choose immediately, by ballot, the President. But in choosing the President, the votes shall be taken by states, the representation from each state having one vote; a quorum for this purpose shall consist of a member or members from two-thirds of the states, and a majority of all the states shall be necessary to a choice. [And if the House of Representatives shall not choose a President whenever the right of choice shall devolve upon them, before the fourth day of March next following, then the Vice-President shall act as President, as in case of the death or other constitutional disability of the President. —]* The person having the greatest number of votes as Vice-President, shall be the Vice-President, if such number be a majority of the whole number of Electors appointed, and if no person have a majority, then from the two highest numbers on the list, the Senate shall choose the Vice-President; a quorum for the purpose shall consist of two-thirds of the whole number of Senators, and a majority of the whole number shall be necessary to a choice. But no person constitutionally ineligible to the office of President shall be eligible to that of Vice-President of the United States. *Superseded by section 3 of the 20th amendment.

AMENDMENT XIII

Passed by Congress January 31, 1865. Ratified December 6, 1865.

Note: A portion of Article IV, section 2, of the Constitution was superseded by the 13th amendment.

Section 1.

Neither slavery nor involuntary servitude, except as a punishment for crime whereof the party shall have been duly convicted, shall exist within the United States, or any place subject to their jurisdiction.

Section 2.

Congress shall have power to enforce this article by appropriate legislation.

AMENDMENT XIV

Passed by Congress June 13, 1866. Ratified July 9, 1868.
Note: Article I, section 2, of the Constitution was modified by section 2 of the 14th amendment.

Section 1.

All persons born or naturalized in the United States, and subject to the jurisdiction thereof, are citizens of the United States and of the State wherein they reside. No State shall make or enforce any law which shall abridge the privileges or immunities of citizens of the United States; nor shall any State deprive any person of life, liberty, or property, without due process of law; nor deny to any person within its jurisdiction the equal protection of the laws.

Section 2.

Representatives shall be apportioned among the several States according to their respective numbers, counting the whole number of persons in each State, excluding Indians not taxed. But when the right to vote at any election for the choice of electors for President and Vice-President of the United States, Representatives in Congress, the Executive and Judicial officers of a State, or the members of the Legislature thereof, is denied to any of the male inhabitants of such State, being twenty-one years of age,* and citizens of the United States, or in any way abridged, except for participation in rebellion, or other crime, the basis of representation therein shall be reduced in the proportion which the number of such male citizens shall bear to the whole number of male citizens twenty-one years of age in such State.

Section 3.

No person shall be a Senator or Representative in Congress, or elector of President and Vice-President, or hold any office, civil or military, under the United States, or under any State, who, having previously taken an oath, as a member of Congress, or as an officer of the United States, or as a member of any State legislature, or as an executive or judicial officer of any State, to support the Constitution of the United States, shall have engaged in insurrection or rebellion against the same, or given aid or comfort to the enemies thereof. But Congress may by a vote of two-thirds of each House, remove such disability.

Section 4.

The validity of the public debt of the United States, authorized by law, including debts incurred for payment of pensions and bounties for services in suppressing insurrection or rebellion, shall not be questioned. But neither the United States nor any State shall assume or pay any debt or obligation incurred in aid of insurrection or rebellion against the United States, or any claim for the loss or emancipation of any slave; but all such debts, obligations and claims shall be held illegal and void.

Section 5.

The Congress shall have power to enforce, by appropriate legislation, the provisions of this article.
Changed by section 1 of the 26th amendment.

AMENDMENT XV

Passed by Congress February 26, 1869. Ratified February 3, 1870.

Section 1.

The right of citizens of the United States to vote shall not be denied or abridged by the United States or by any State on account of race, color, or previous condition of servitude—

Section 2.

The Congress shall have power to enforce this article by appropriate legislation.

AMENDMENT XVI

Passed by Congress July 2, 1909. Ratified February 3, 1913.

Note: Article I, section 9, of the Constitution was modified by amendment 16.

The Congress shall have power to lay and collect taxes on incomes, from whatever source derived, without apportionment among the several States, and without regard to any census or enumeration.

AMENDMENT XVII

Passed by Congress May 13, 1912. Ratified April 8, 1913.

Note: Article I, section 3, of the Constitution was modified by the 17th amendment.

The Senate of the United States shall be composed of two Senators from each State, elected by the people thereof, for six years; and each Senator shall have one vote. The electors in each State shall have the qualifications requisite for electors of the most numerous branch of the State legislatures.

When vacancies happen in the representation of any State in the Senate, the executive authority of such State shall issue writs of election to fill such vacancies: Provided, That the legislature of any State may empower the executive thereof to make temporary appointments until the people fill the vacancies by election as the legislature may direct.

This amendment shall not be so construed as to affect the election or term of any Senator chosen before it becomes valid as part of the Constitution.

AMENDMENT XVIII

Passed by Congress December 18, 1917. Ratified January 16, 1919. Repealed by amendment 21.

Section 1.

After one year from the ratification of this article the manufacture, sale, or transportation of intoxicating liquors within, the importation thereof into, or the exportation thereof from the United States and all territory subject to the jurisdiction thereof for beverage purposes is hereby prohibited.

Section 2.

The Congress and the several States shall have concurrent power to enforce this article by appropriate legislation.

Section 3.

This article shall be inoperative unless it shall have been ratified as an amendment to the Constitution by the legislatures of the several States, as provided in the Constitution, within seven years from the date of the submission hereof to the States by the Congress.

AMENDMENT XIX

Passed by Congress June 4, 1919. Ratified August 18, 1920.

The right of citizens of the United States to vote shall not be denied or abridged by the United States or by any State on account of sex.

Congress shall have power to enforce this article by appropriate legislation.

AMENDMENT XX

Passed by Congress March 2, 1932. Ratified January 23, 1933.

Note: Article I, section 4, of the Constitution was modified by section 2 of this amendment. In addition, a portion of the 12th amendment was superseded by section 3.

Section 1.

The terms of the President and the Vice President shall end at noon on the 20th day of January, and the terms of Senators and Representatives at noon on the 3d day of January, of the years in which such terms would have ended if this article had not been ratified; and the terms of their successors shall then begin.

Section 2.

The Congress shall assemble at least once in every year, and such meeting shall begin at noon on the 3d day of January, unless they shall by law appoint a different day.

Section 3.

If, at the time fixed for the beginning of the term of the President, the President elect shall have died, the Vice President elect shall become President. If a President shall not have been chosen before the time fixed for the beginning of his term, or if the President elect shall have failed to qualify, then the Vice President elect shall act as President until a President shall have qualified; and the Congress may by law provide for the case wherein neither a President elect nor a Vice President elect shall have qualified, declaring who shall then act as President, or the manner in which one who is to act shall be selected, and such person shall act accordingly until a President or Vice President shall have qualified.

Section 4.

The Congress may by law provide for the case of the death of any of the persons from whom the House of Representatives may choose a President whenever the right of choice shall have devolved upon them, and for the case of the death of any of the persons from whom the Senate may choose a Vice President whenever the right of choice shall have devolved upon them.

Section 5.

Sections 1 and 2 shall take effect on the 15th day of October following the ratification of this article.

Section 6.

This article shall be inoperative unless it shall have been ratified as an amendment to the Constitution by the legislatures of three-fourths of the several States within seven years from the date of its submission.

AMENDMENT XXI

Passed by Congress February 20, 1933. Ratified December 5, 1933.

Section 1.

The eighteenth article of amendment to the Constitution of the United States is hereby repealed.

Section 2.

The transportation or importation into any State, Territory, or possession of the United States for delivery or use therein of intoxicating liquors, in violation of the laws thereof, is hereby prohibited.

Section 3.

This article shall be inoperative unless it shall have been ratified as an amendment to the Constitution by conventions in the several States, as provided in the Constitution, within seven years from the date of the submission hereof to the States by the Congress.

AMENDMENT XXII

Passed by Congress March 21, 1947. Ratified February 27, 1951.

Section 1.

No person shall be elected to the office of the President more than twice, and no person who has held the office of President, or acted as President, for more than two years of a term to which some other person was elected President shall be elected to the office of the President more than once. But this Article shall not apply to any person holding the office of President when this Article was proposed by the Congress, and shall not prevent any person who may be holding the office of President, or acting as President, during the term within which this Article becomes operative from holding the office of President or acting as President during the remainder of such term.

Section 2.

This article shall be inoperative unless it shall have been ratified as an amendment to the Constitution by the legislatures of three-fourths of the several States within seven years from the date of its submission to the States by the Congress.

AMENDMENT XXIII

Passed by Congress June 16, 1960. Ratified March 29, 1961.

Section 1.

The District constituting the seat of Government of the United States shall appoint in such manner as the Congress may direct:

A number of electors of President and Vice President equal to the whole number of Senators and Representatives in Congress to which the District would be entitled if it were a State, but in no event more than the least populous State; they shall be in addition to those appointed by the States, but they shall be considered, for the purposes of the election of President and Vice President, to be electors appointed by a State; and they shall meet in the District and perform such duties as provided by the twelfth article of amendment.

Section 2.

The Congress shall have power to enforce this article by appropriate legislation.

AMENDMENT XXIV

Passed by Congress August 27, 1962. Ratified January 23, 1964.

Section 1.

The right of citizens of the United States to vote in any primary or other election for President or Vice President, for electors for President or Vice President, or for Senator or Representative in Congress, shall not be denied or abridged by the United States or any State by reason of failure to pay any poll tax or other tax.

Section 2.

The Congress shall have power to enforce this article by appropriate legislation.

AMENDMENT XXV

Passed by Congress July 6, 1965. Ratified February 10, 1967.

Note: Article II, section 1, of the Constitution was affected by the 25th amendment.

Section 1.

In case of the removal of the President from office or of his death or resignation, the Vice President shall become President.

Section 2.

Whenever there is a vacancy in the office of the Vice President, the President shall nominate a Vice President who shall take office upon confirmation by a majority vote of both Houses of Congress.

Section 3.

Whenever the President transmits to the President pro tempore of the Senate and the Speaker of the House of Representatives his written declaration that he is unable to discharge the powers and duties of his office, and until he transmits to them a written declaration to the contrary, such powers and duties shall be discharged by the Vice President as Acting President.

Section 4.

Whenever the Vice President and a majority of either the principal officers of the executive departments or of such other body as Congress may by law provide, transmit to the President pro tempore of the Senate and the Speaker of the House of Representatives their written declaration that the President is unable to discharge the powers and duties of his office, the Vice President shall immediately assume the powers and duties of the office as Acting President.

Thereafter, when the President transmits to the President pro tempore of the Senate and the Speaker of the House of Representatives his written declaration that no inability exists, he shall resume the powers and duties of his office unless the Vice President and a majority of either the principal officers of the executive department or of such other body as Congress may by law provide, transmit within four days to the President pro tempore of the Senate and the Speaker of the House of Representatives their written declaration that the President is unable to discharge the powers and duties of his office. Thereupon Congress shall decide the issue, assembling within forty-eight hours for that purpose if not in session. If the Congress, within twenty-one days after receipt of the latter written declaration, or, if Congress is not in session, within twenty-one days after Congress is required to assemble, determines by two-thirds vote of both Houses that the President is unable to discharge the powers and duties of his office, the Vice President shall continue to discharge the same as Acting President; otherwise, the President shall resume the powers and duties of his office.

AMENDMENT XXVI

Passed by Congress March 23, 1971. Ratified July 1, 1971.
Note: Amendment 14, section 2, of the Constitution was modified by section 1 of the 26th amendment.

Section 1.

The right of citizens of the United States, who are eighteen years of age or older, to vote shall not be denied or abridged by the United States or by any State on account of age.

Section 2.

The Congress shall have power to enforce this article by appropriate legislation.

AMENDMENT XXVII

Originally proposed Sept. 25, 1789. Ratified May 7, 1992.
No law, varying the compensation for the services of the Senators and Representatives, shall take effect, until an election of Representatives shall have intervened.

Made in the USA
Columbia, SC
05 June 2025